Start Scrapbooking

Your essential guide to recording memories

Wendy Smedley

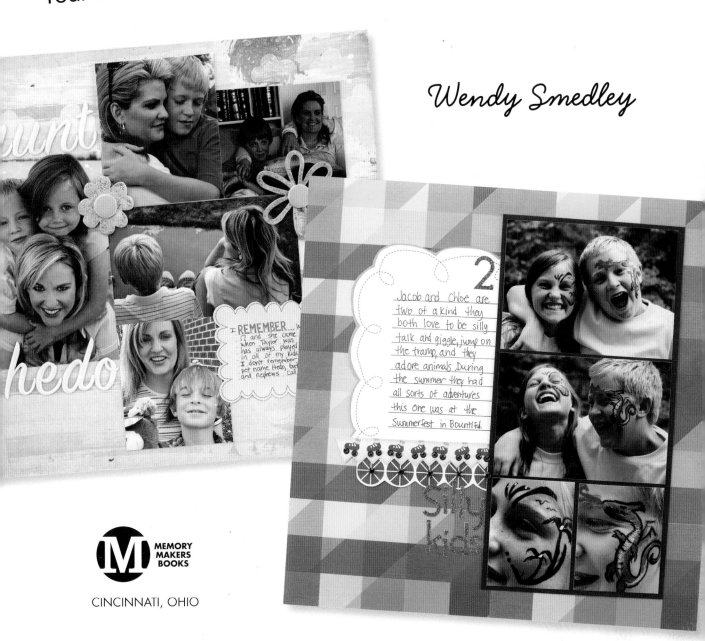

MEMORY MAKERS BOOKS

CINCINNATI, OHIO

14 13 12 11 10   5 4 3 2

Distributed in Canada by Fraser Direct
100 Armstrong Avenue
Georgetown, ON, Canada L7G 5S4
Tel: (905) 877-4411

Distributed in the U.K. and Europe by David & Charles
Brunel House, Newton Abbot, Devon, TQ12 4PU, England
Tel: (+44) 1626 323200, Fax: (+44) 1626 323319
E-mail: postmaster@davidandcharles.co.uk

Distributed in Australia by Capricorn Link
P.O. Box 704, S. Windsor, NSW 2756 Australia
Tel: (02) 4577-3555

Library of Congress Cataloging-in-Publication Data

Smedley, Wendy.
  Start scrapbooking : your essential guide to recording memories / Wendy Smedley.
      p. cm.
  Includes index.
  ISBN 978-1-59963-128-8 (alk. paper)
  1. Photograph albums. 2. Scrapbooking. I. Title.
  TR501.S58 2010
  745.593–dc22

                                  2010005430

Editor: *Kristin Boys*
Designer: *Steven Peters*
Production Coordinator: *Greg Nock*
Photographers: *Christine Polomsky, Al Parrish*
Stylist: *Jan Nickum*

fw media
www.fwmedia.com

Metric Conversion Chart

to convert	to	multiply by
Inches	Centimeters	2.54
Centimeters	Inches	0.4
Feet	Centimeters	30.5
Centimeters	Feet	0.03
Yards	Meters	0.9
Meters	Yards	1.1

Wendy Smedley was the creative editor for *Simple Scrapbooks* magazine for more than five years. She is the author of *The Complete Idiot's Guide to Scrapbooking* and, more recently, the coauthor of *The Organized and Inspired Scrapbooker*. Smedley, who calls Utah home, has been a frequent guest host for the PBS TV show, *Scrapbook Memories* and is a certified veteran of industrial retail trade shows. She has taught classes on memory-keeping internationally. When not journaling, cutting or cropping, Smedley enjoys reading good books, photographing her family, independent cinema and spending time with her husband, Kent, five boys and an assortment of animals.

Dedication

I appreciate my mom's oldest sister, Virgie Day, for leading the way in uncovering our family history and instilling in my mom, Patsy, the idea that you can accomplish anything with determination and hard work.

Additional acknowledgments go to:
My parents, for their collective example of unwavering honesty.
My husband, Kent, and five sons, for providing me with both material and inspiration for my scrapbooking projects and for tolerating my photo-taking whims and crafting messes.
My circle of friends. Thank you for your support and words of encouragement.
My brother, Shawn, for pushing me to examine different perspectives and cultures, and encouraging my quest for knowledge.

And thanks to all of the gifted staff at F+W Media who have lent their expertise to this book.

Acknowledgments

To my friends and colleagues in the scrapbooking industry whose relationships I value. This is my way of growing and supporting this industry I love.

To scrapbookers all over the world who have befriended me and shared their stories with not only me but the world.

To anyone who has ever endeavored to chronicle, in any form, the great adventure that is life.

And finally, this book is dedicated to you, the reader. Let me commend you for your willingness to give this hobby a chance, and congratulations to you for trying something new. Now get busy!

Contributing Artists

Thank you to the following artists who contributed work to the book:

Elizabeth Dillow
Cheyenne, WY

Monica McNeil
Dallas, TX

Katrina Simeck
Colchester, VT

Lain Ehmann
Lexington, MA

Amber Packer
Sandy, UT

Celeste Smith
West Hartford, CT

Rachel Gainer
Saratoga Springs, UT

Emily Pitts
Thornton, CO

Elisha Snow
Farmington, UT

Paula Gilarde
Bedford, MA

Beth Proudfoot
Lebanon, NJ

Cathy Zielske
St. Paul, MN

Angie Lucas
Sandy, UT

Contents

Welcome to Scrapbooking!

What is this hobby you have heard so much about? Why does it matter? And what is all the fuss about?

Well, scrapbooking is a blend of crafting and storytelling, photography and love that turns ordinary photos and words into a manifestation of your life. It's time well spent creating, sharing stories and preserving your memories.

If you've picked up this book, you're no doubt interested in doing something with your photos. Like most of us, you probably have thousands of photos (some in boxes, but most stored on your hard drive), which is driving your motivation to scrapbook. The good news is that you don't have to (and really shouldn't) scrap every photo. Scrapbooking provides a creative outlet for organizing and focusing on recording specific memories—and what kinds of memories to document is completely up to you. In fact, one of the best things about scrapbooking is that there are very few rules. Why you scrapbook, what topics you cover and how you complete the process is up to you. Everyone can follow her own individual scrapbook journey.

Start Scrapbooking is your guide to getting started in this wonderful craft. Inside these pages, I'll help you determine your goals for scrapbooking and how you will go about accomplishing them. I'll show you all the tools you'll need to have and the products to have fun with, and teach you how to use them. You'll learn the basics of telling your story and how to effectively convey those stories using basic design principles. Finally, I'll give you a gallery of layouts organized by theme to get you started on your way. As you flip through the book the first time, look at the visuals and get excited, then start at the beginning and read, take notes, think about the content and be ready to join the world of scrapbookers in celebrating life on paper.

Welcome to the world of scrapbooking, a place where ordinary photos and words become extraordinary symbols of your life.

KIDS

goals
1. record holidays
2. celebrate relationships
3. chronicle childhood

Chapter One

Why Scrapbook?

In its simplest terms, scrapbooking is memory keeping—the act of pairing photographs and words in a decorative fashion. The way or style in which you do this can be as simple or as elaborate as you imagine. With the onset of digital photography, the lofty goal of scrapbooking every photograph is vanishing because it is next to impossible to accomplish with the amount of photos we are taking now. The flexibility of the craft coupled with the need to narrow our focus means that everyone has different goals for scrapbooking. Perhaps you want to record your children's young lives while your friend intends to preserve her family's heritage. Someone else might simply want to dress up photos with pretty paper. You also may have more than one goal. As you get more into the craft you will likely redefine your goals often. For now, keep reading to help you determine why you want to scrapbook. I've included the top ten reasons people scrapbook to give you a starting point in determining your own intentions.

Why I Scrapbook

I started scrapbooking as a way to organize my photos. I still appreciate this benefit of scrapbooking, but my purposes have changed. I scrapbook for the creative and social outlet. I scrapbook to tell my family's stories. I scrapbook to express my perspective regarding my everyday life. And I scrapbook to acknowledge and celebrate my life. All of my loved ones benefit from my scrapbooking; each of my five children enjoys looking at photos of their childhood, remembering holidays and favorite vacations and reading about my own childhood memories. This hobby is both fulfilling and educational. I have become more knowledgeable about photography and design by improving my scrapbooking skills.

🌼 *Reason #1* 🌼
Record Family Holidays

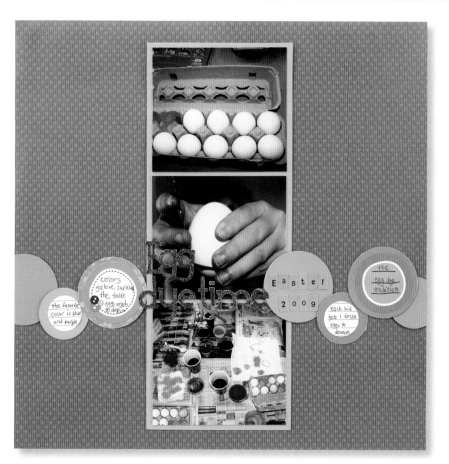

The playful use of circles mimics the shape of the eggs, the main subject of this layout, which highlights the tradition of egg dyeing. Photos of the supplies used in this family tradition give context and color to the story and share a different point of view.

Supplies: patterned paper (Bo Bunny); letters (KI Memories, My Little Shoebox); stickers (American Crafts); pen (American Crafts); Misc: circle punch

With photos of me from three different decades, this layout expresses what I want to discover through scrapbooking. The pink and black floral accents promote a feminine air and repeat the colors of the papers, solidifying the design. The informal yet informative journaling list describes basic desires in an easy-to-write format.

Supplies: cardstock (Bazzill); flowers, brads (Making Memories)

Determining Your Goals

It's not absolutely neccessary to determine your goals for scrapbooking before you start, but doing so will help you focus your attention and keep you from getting overwhelmed by all that "must" be done. Often, searching for a starting point is the hardest part of scrapbooking. So figuring out your goals—who you want to take photos of, what subjects you want to remember, what products you want to use—narrows the search and provides a starting point for determining how you will scrapbook the who and what. I recommend that you be deliberate about determining your goals for the first few projects you start. Use the Project Goals Worksheet on page 17 to record your goals. After you go through this process a few times, it will become second nature to you. Soon you will constantly consider how to make layouts that support your overall goals.

Why Do You Want to Scrapbook?

What do you want to accomplish by participating in this hobby? You may be wondering why this question is even relevant to ask. You just want to make pretty things! But trust me, it is relevant. In fact, "just wanting to make pretty things" is a reason to scrapbook. You may have different goals at different times and for different projects—that's okay! Keeping in mind your overall goal for scrapbooking will allow you to succeed because you will know what it is you want to achieve before you even begin.

⚙ *Reason #3* ⚙
Showcase Photos

Elisha is a photographer by trade, so it is important for her to understand why she is scrapbooking in order to select which of her hundreds of photos to preserve. She is the mother of three young sons so she focuses on layouts that document her kids' unique personalities. This layout shows that there is no question about whether her son is "absolutely awesome." All it takes is one snapshot to illustrate this toddler's penchant for style.

Supplies: cardstock (Bazzill); letters (American Crafts); brads (Doodlebug Designs); Misc: Century Gothic font

Artwork by *Elisha Snow*

Scrapbooking Communities

In most creative hobbies, there is a desire to share creations, and scrapbooking is no exception. Hundreds of scrapbooking communities populate the Web with online galleries, classes, scrapbook challenges, project tutorials, new product reviews and places to exchange ideas with other scrapbookers.

Scrapbook.com has a gallery that boasts over a million shared layouts as well as hundreds of images of scrapbook spaces, cards and other papercrafts projects. If you are looking for challenges and inspiration, try writeclickscrapbook.com; each month they share a challenge and then post daily inspiration. Also visit memorymakersmagazine.com to share layouts in the Online Idea Gallery and thoughts in the forums.

What Do You Want to Start With?

Once you have in mind an overall goal for scrapbooking, start to determine what you want to scrapbook. Naturally, look to your photographs to get you started. Which photos do you consider important enough to record? What images do you want to add a story to? What do you want more photos of? Popular topics to scrapbook include milestones such as weddings or graduations, holidays and seasons, events such as dance recitals or sports and all kinds of travel from camping to cruising. Many people start scrapbooking to commemorate their loved ones' accolades. Think back to what you know of your parents' childhoods and what you would like to know more about. Asking these questions will guide you in determining what your own scrapbooks will say.

This milestone layout tells the photo story of a cheerful carnival wedding. One of scrapbooking's many appeals is the ability to customize the environment in which your photos are housed. This backyard carnival needed a unique look created from scratch. Surrounded by whimsical heart patterned paper and shiny accents, these four photos show off the happy couple and the cheerful setting.

Supplies: patterned paper, letters (American Crafts); brads (Doodlebug Designs)

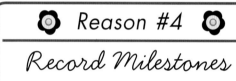

Reason #4

Record Milestones

Scrapbooking her son's activities in the academic group Odyssey of the Minds allows Katrina to proudly feature her son's achievement. Written in a journalistic style, the writing reads like an announcement in today's paper. This keeps the layout interesting and the sentiment less like bragging.

Supplies: cardstock (Bazzill); patterned paper (October Afternoon); letters (American Crafts); brads (Making Memories); Misc: punch

Artwork by *Katrina Simeck*

Who Do You Want to Record?

Who refers to the people, places and things in your photographs. Who do you want to scrapbook? You? Your kids? Your friends? All of the above? You may be surprised to find that you don't have many photos of your parents, for example, or yourself. Solidifying what subjects you want to scrapbook keeps you aware of who to photograph.

❀ Reason #5 ❀
Celebrate Relationships

Looking through old photographs, Angie found images of many of her friends. Gathering these images of friends over the years helped her record special relationships. She trimmed all but the subjects and placed them side by side to create a double-page layout. The journaling explains how important her friends are to her and when she met them.

Supplies: cardstock (Bazzill); accents (OScrap); letters (Karen Foster); pen (American Crafts)

Artwork by *Angie Lucas*

Looking at photos of the same subject spread over a few years allows you to clearly see how much that person has changed. This is especially true with children because they change so drastically. Showcasing my son Justin over a period of time brings his personality to the forefront. He has a penchant for friends, and people are instantly drawn to him.

Supplies: cardstock (DCWV); patterned paper (BasicGrey, October Afternoon); letters (American Crafts); circle tag (Making Memories)

❀ Reason #6 ❀
Chronicle Childhood

Where and When Will You Scrapbook?

Preconceiving the physical space where you are going to scrapbook will help you determine the type of storage to purchase for your supplies. Will you be scrapbooking at home? If so, will you have a dedicated space where you can leave supplies out? Will you be using a shared space and need to clean everything up each time you scrapbook? Do you plan to scrapbook on the go? Determining the place you will scrapbook and preparing it properly will eliminate frustration and allow you to focus on the task at hand. (See page 39 for more on organizing your workspace.)

Determining when you will scrapbook will help you plan how many projects you can complete, and also ensure that you will actually make time to scrapbook. Often it helps to schedule time to scrapbook with others; you can do this by participating in a monthly group with friends or attending weekly crops at your local scrapbook store. Knowing people are counting on you to show will encourage you to scrapbook. I also recommend scheduling time to scrap by yourself—for example, make every Thursday morning scrapbook time. You can also make time for scrapping by dividing the tasks for a page. For example, spend one session editing and printing photos for a handful of layouts, then spend the next session planning the design and gathering products and tools.

⊙ Reason #7 ⊙
Commemorate Achievements

You can create an effective space for scrapping even in just a corner of a room. Keep supplies at hand and organized on your desk using jars and tins. A bulletin board provides a space for inspiration and for organizing ideas and schedules. Keep your favorite books in your space for easy access to design ideas. A small shelf above your desk provides additional storage opportunity in even the tightest spaces.

How Will You Achieve These Goals?

This is where you answer the question of how you are going to execute the why, what and who of the above. Are you going to create one layout on the topic, several pages or a whole album? Is there a special product you want to use in a project? Or perhaps there is a new technique you want to try on a layout. If so, do you have the right tools and supplies? Thinking about how you will scrapbook will ensure you have what you need to succeed.

❀ *Reason #8* ❀

Express Personal Thoughts

The two photographs of handmade quilts shine on this minimalist layout. The photos are colorful and full of patterns, so I wanted to keep the product contrast to a minimum. In order to accomplish this, I looked for background paper and letter stickers that were similar in color for a monochromatic look. In addition, the wrapped trim around the photos holds a tiny tag that lists what each quilt was made for. The heart patterned paper repeats the cross-stitch design, giving it a handmade feel and making it a great choice for this layout.

Supplies: cardstock, patterned paper (American Crafts); letters (American Crafts, My Little Shoebox); journaling card (Jenni Bowlin); Misc: ribbon, tags

---

❀ *Reason #9* ❀

Partake in the Creative Process

There are many hows behind each layout. This one represents a myriad of choices: first locating the photos and copying them, second selecting products that complement the older photos, then deciding what direction to take with journaling. A vintage patterned paper correlates to the age of the photos, and matting them in black emphasizes their importance. Keeping the design centered, the flower and trim separate the photo from the journaling.

Supplies: cardstock (Provo Craft); patterned paper, sticker (Pink Paislee); letters (American Crafts)

Project Goals Worksheet

Copy this worksheet prior to beginning your first few layouts. Answering the questions will help you determine your goals and provide a starting point for scrapbooking.

Project name: _____

My overall goal(s) for scrapbooking: _____

What topic do I want to scrapbook in this project? _____

Who do I want to feature in this project? _____

How will I accomplish these goals?
    Single layout _____
    Multiple layouts _____
    Album _____

Products I would like to use: _____

Techniques I would like to try: _____

Chapter Two

Setting Up Shop

I started scrapbooking by attending a weekly workshop at my local scrapbook store. Not only did it provide connections to other scrapbookers, the workshop allowed me to try tools and materials before I purchased them, which in turn helped me to buy only what I would actually use. All of this was important given that there was (and still is) a multitude of tools and materials to potentially own. Veteran scrapbookers often become a bit obsessed with all the lovely scrapbook materials at their fingertips, but for newcomers the choices can be overwhelming. For me, opening up a new package of paper or brads is exciting, and I want you to find delight in buying supplies as well. Read on to learn about the range of scrapbooking tools and materials, and to decide for yourself how you will build your scrapbooking toolbox.

Tools of the Trade

The availability and variety of scrapbooking tools has grown dramatically in the last few years. But to get started, you really need only a few basics: something to cut with, adhesive and a pen. Below I've outlined the tools that are staples for scrapbookers. Take a look and see what might suit you best.

Cutting Tools

PAPER TRIMMER

I still use the same type of paper trimmer I did when I first started scrapbooking (you tend to grow attached to certain tools). Technically, all you need to cut paper and photos are scissors, but a paper trimmer really is a must-have. With its ability to cut straight lines with ease, using a paper trimmer will make your scrapping life so much easier. The difference between the three types of paper trimmers is mainly the blade type.

This layout's clean, straight lines are the result of cutting with a paper trimmer. Using a paper trimmer is especially important with thin strips , such as the stripe here, as any uneven edges are more obvious. A naturalistic design along with masculine colors affirms the theme and subjects of this layout. A bit of journaling calls attention to details of a trip to Yellowstone Park.

Supplies: cardstock (Provo Craft); patterned paper (BasicGrey); letters (Doodlebug Designs); pen (Sakura)

Essential Tool Kit

Keep organized by grouping the essential tools and keeping them close at hand. In my essential kit I keep the following:

- paper trimmer
- small scissors
- liquid adhesive
- dry adhesive
- clear acrylic ruler
- pencil
- art gum eraser
- corner rounder

ROTARY

This blade rolls inside a cartridge that protects you from getting cut. You can cut more than one sheet of paper at a time without tearing them. The benefit of the rotary blade is that you can switch the blade for different edge styles such as switching from a plain edge to a scallop edge.

STRAIGHT

Straight trimmers are the least expensive to purchase but also cut only one or two pages at once. They're easy to use for beginners and the blade can be replaced when it becomes dull.

GUILLOTINE

A guillotine blade is attached to an armlike handle. To cut, you lower the arm. This blade provides a very sharp, clean cut. Because the blade is so sharp, you will want to purchase a trimmer with a locking device to keep little fingers out of harm's way.

When deciding which trimmer to purchase, make sure the cutting plate fits at least 12" (30cm) of paper. (Many trimmers have an extended ruler arm so you can measure out to 12" [30cm].) Another thing to consider is where you will do your scrapbooking: If you plan to scrapbook on the go or have a small workspace, portability will be an important feature for you.

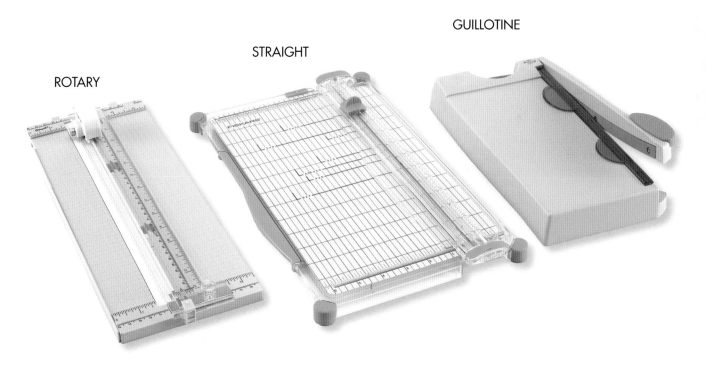

GUILLOTINE

STRAIGHT

ROTARY

SCISSORS

You might assume that scissors and paper trimmers do the same job, but that's not quite true. Paper trimmers are your best bet for cutting straight lines, but you'll need a pair (or multiple!) of scissors for cutting everything else.

STRAIGHT-EDGE SCISSORS

Straight-edge scissors with sharp blades are great for basic cutting, and the sharp blade is also great for cutting ribbon and trim. Those with short blades and sharp tips are my favorite. The small blade size works well for cutting shapes and working in tight corners. Avoid purchasing any pair of scissors that are too expensive because after a while your blades will get dull and you will want to replace them.

DECORATIVE-EDGE SCISSORS

One of the first tools the infant scrapbooking community embraced was a pair of decorative-edge scissors. With options like deckle, scallop and zigzag, they're still going strong today. I suggest avoiding the temptation to use these scissors on your photos, and instead save them for adding interest to patterned paper and cardstock.

CRAFT KNIFE

A craft knife is not a must-have for your tool kit, but many scrappers swear by this tool. A craft knife's sharp blade can make precision cuts, which is helpful for cutting out patterns from paper as well as other precise cutting tasks.

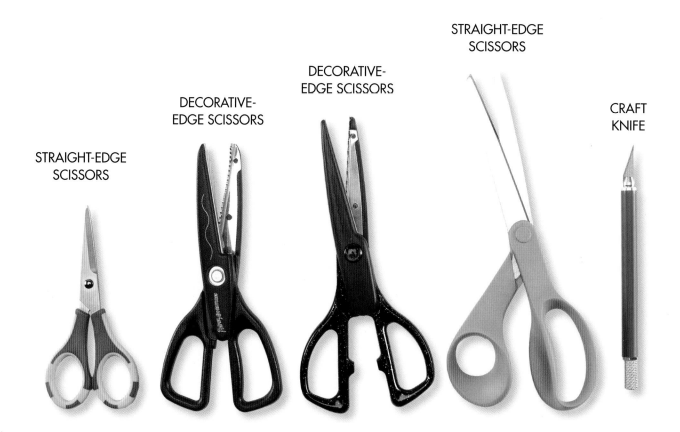

STRAIGHT-EDGE
SCISSORS

DECORATIVE-
EDGE SCISSORS

DECORATIVE-
EDGE SCISSORS

STRAIGHT-EDGE
SCISSORS

CRAFT
KNIFE

It's possible to use bold patterned paper on a layout without overwhelming the design. Just trim the paper with a pair of decorative-edge scissors, creating your own stylish border. Keep the rest of the layout uncluttered by cutting all the photos to the same size and creating a colorful, yet simple title. Pull together the finishing touches quickly by using prestitched buttons and one of your favorite quotes for journaling.

Supplies: cardstock, patterned paper (American Crafts); buttons (Sassafras Lass); letters (Making Memories); Misc: Blackjack font

If we had no winter, the spring would not be so pleasant: if we did not sometimes taste of adversity, prosperity would not be so welcome. —Anne Bradstreet

Create Your Own Trims With Decorative-Edge Scissors

With decorative-edge scissors you can make trim from your favorite papers to match any layout.

MATERIALS LIST
patterned paper, decorative-edge scissors, ruler, pencil

1. Cut along the edge of your paper with the decorative-edge scissors. Be careful to match up the pattern with each cut you make.

2. Turn the paper over, and measure and mark the width of the trim.

3. Cut along the line with the decorative-edge scissors.

PUNCHES

Imagine being able to craft perfect circles, cupcakes or scalloped borders. You can achieve just that with ease using paper punches. Punches range in shape from simple to complex, and they come in a variety of sizes, from ½" (1cm) shapes to 2" (5cm) or larger. You can also find border punches to craft pretty decorative edges, and simple corner rounders provide an easy finished edge. Choose a versatile shape, like a circle or square to get started.

Add Pizzazz with a Border Punch

A fancy border punch can jazz up a basic journaling block. A lace border provides both texture and dimension with color peeking through the punched holes.

MATERIALS LIST
paper trimmer, border punch, patterned paper

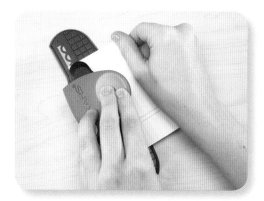

1. Cut patterned paper to the desired size for journaling. Starting in the center of the bottom of the journaling block, punch the border. (Note: Beginning in the center will ensure that you end with the same part of the punched design at each edge.)

2. Slide the paper to the left or the right, line up with the punched pattern, and punch again. Continue this until the entire bottom border is punched.

This simple, monochromatic design puts all the focus on my son's love for animals, especially these darling puppies. Enhancing the journaling with a border punch gives the simple layout some pizzazz. A few textured accents provide a bit more dimension without distracting from the subject matter.

Supplies: cardstock (Prism); letters (Luxe Designs); patterned paper (Scenic Route); trim (Making Memories); circle tag (Pebbles Inc.); Misc: border punch, brad

Quick Tip

You can sharpen dull punches by punching them through a sheet of aluminum foil.

DIE-CUTTING MACHINES

Die-cutting machines allow you to cut designs out of paper (and other materials). Available in manual or electronic versions, these are popular tools with scrapbookers because of the variety of designs available. Keep in mind that along with the machine you will need to purchase the design templates or cartridges.

MANUAL DIE-CUTTING MACHINES

A manual die-cutting machine works by sandwiching a die and paper in the machine and manually cranking it through. Some of the dies have the ability to emboss and cut at the same time.

ELECTRONIC DIE-CUTTING MACHINES

Electronic machines give you more choices than manual because you can vary the size of the shape (depending on the options of your machine). Electronic machines store shapes digitally, either on a cartridge or on the computer. The features vary on these machines so make sure you are certain what you want your machine to do before you buy.

MANUAL DIE-CUTTING MACHINE

ELECTRONIC DIE-CUTTING MACHINE

Quick Tip

Invest in a basic alphabet die set. This will be a set you use over and over again.

Die-Cutting Machines

Electronic
Slice by Making Memories
Cricut by Provo Craft
Creative Cutter by Pazzles
SD Digital Craft Cutter by QuicKutz

Manual
Cuttlebug by Provo Craft
Sizzix by Ellison
Epic by QuicKutz
The Wizard by Spellbinders

ADHESIVE

A large assortment of adhesives handles your scrapbooking needs, including basic adhesive for paper and photos and specialty adhesives like vellum tape, removable adhesive and photo squares. Choosing adhesive can seem overwhelming, but if you read the labels, you'll figure out what type is best for what purpose. Everyone has a favorite adhesive, so try out a few until you find the one(s) you like. I suggest using two types of adhesive: dry adhesive for photos and paper and liquid or specialty adhesive for accents.

WET ADHESIVES

Liquid glue is great to use with ribbon, fabric and other soft embellishments because it adheres quickly and holds strongly. Glue sticks work great for large chipboard accents and other thick embellishments. Plus, it's easy to control the amount of adhesive you use with a glue stick.

DRY ADHESIVES

Dry adhesives include adhesive runners as well as double-sided tape and photo corners. They all work similarly, so choose what you prefer. Dry adhesive is best for photos and paper because it won't bleed through. It's less messy than liquid glue and comes in both permanent and repositionable formulas. I recommend using a refillable adhesive runner because it is simple to apply and can be used to adhere paper, photos and nondimensional accents.

SPECIALTY ADHESIVES

When working with embellishments, speciality adhesives can do the job better than typical dry or wet adhesive. Adhesive dots (like Glue Dots), which have high tack, are great for adhering materials like plastic and metal. Adhesive strips make attaching delicate trim a snap. When you want to add dimension to basic paper embellishments, adhesive foam gives you a lift.

LIQUID GLUE

GLUE STICK

DOUBLE-SIDED TAPE

ADHESIVE RUNNERS

ADHESIVE STRIPS

ADHESIVE FOAM

Have liquid glue on hand for adhering accents like this chipboard flower. If you don't like liquid glue, you can use a glue stick for these types of products. Also have an adhesive runner for attaching paper, like the trim and journaling block I added on this page.

Supplies: patterned paper, stickers (BasicGrey); chipboard flower (Pebbles Inc); pen (EK Success)

Adhere Photos Quickly and Securely

As a scrapbooker, you will adhere endless amounts of photos, and you will want to do so quickly and efficiently. Using an adhesive runner helps speed up the task.

MATERIALS LIST
photo (with mat optional), adhesive runner

On the back of the photo (or photo mat), press the tip of the adhesive runner. Drag and then lift to transfer a small strip of adhesive to one corner. Repeat to apply adhesive to each corner.

ADDITIONAL TOOLS

Cutting tools and adhesive are must-haves for the most basic of scrapbooking tasks. But there are many more tools you can purchase to help with a variety of jobs. Below are those that I find most useful to have on hand.

WRITING TOOLS

Whether you are handwriting journaling or outlining letters, you will want to have **scrapbook pens** in your tool kit. Product manufacturers make a variety of pens with different tip sizes, colors and ink types for varying surfaces (and because they are intended for scrapbooking, you can be sure they are safe for your layouts). Your first pen purchases should be neutral colors. Also keep in your tool kit a **pencil** and **art gum eraser**. Writing and sketching in pencil first is always a good way to eliminate mistakes. An art gum eraser removes pencil marks cleanly and over pen without smearing the ink.

MEASURING TOOLS

A **ruler** is essential for drawing straight lines and for perfectly aligning titles and elements. **Cutting mats** provide a protective surface when using a paper piercer or craft knife. Most mats have grid lines to aid in measuring, and many are magnetic, which makes it easy to keep metal rulers in place.

OTHER TOOLS

Walking through a scrapbook or craft store, you will discover many other specialty tools. Whenever possible, try before you buy; you don't want to be stuck storing tools you rarely use. These are some of my favorites to have on hand: a sturdy **rub-on applicator** will allow your rub-ons to go on smoothly and help you avoid mistakes. When working with little embellishments, **tweezers** are handy for picking up or holding while you glue. A **Crop-A-Dile** is a mighty tool to quickly set eyelets and punch holes through chipboard with ease. A **paper piercer** is good for poking holes through layers of paper, especially in the middle of a layout, where a regular hole punch won't reach.

You can make simple products extra-special with specialty pens. Use a white pen like the one used here to outline colored chipboard letters and make them pop. Finish off the layout with handwritten journaling done with a black pen.

Supplies: cardstock (Bazzill); patterned paper, rub-ons (Colorbok); letters, acrylic stars (Heidi Swapp); pens (Sharpie, Sakura)

Products to Play With

Products are the fun part of scrapbooking: the pretty papers, cute embellishments, stamped images and gorgeous trim. These products support the theme or mood of your layout. When starting to scrapbook, look for consumable products that will work on a variety of pages, such as basic brads, label stamps or black letter stickers.

PAPER

A complete necessity, all scrapbookers have a love affair with paper. The two basic types, plain cardstock and patterned paper, are equally useful on a page. Papers are available in every color and pattern imaginable and in different weights and shapes.

CARDSTOCK

With hundreds of colors and numerous textures to choose from, cardstock is easy to work with and inexpensive. Plain cardstock is typically reserved for making a sturdy, unfussy background for a layout, but you can also use cardstock to mat photos, cover chipboard, create custom die-cuts and more.

PATTERNED PAPER

From flowers and balloons to stripes and damask and everything in between, the different patterns available in patterned paper are seemingly endless. Even if you're looking for a little glitz you will find it: Many patterned papers have texture such as glitter, flock and foil. Patterned papers also make highlighting themes simple. Available in traditional 12" × 12" (30cm × 30cm) size as well as in shapes like circles and stars, or with decorative edges, you're sure to find a patterned paper (or a hundred!) that's a favorite.

The bright and upbeat patterns used on this layout reinforce the emotive message in the journaling. Notice that cardstock is the foundation for the pieces of paper and photo. Also, the journaling and title are printed directly onto cardstock, which makes for a clean and uncluttered design.

Supplies: patterned paper, rub-ons (American Crafts); Misc: Georgia font

Artwork by *Beth Proudfoot*

Sporting their favorite new shirts, my sons Jacob and Nathan are ready, if somewhat reluctant, to go back to school. The theme is communicated in the word patterned paper. Mixing different patterns of paper works when colors coordinate and there is a mix of pattern sizes. Notice how the colors in the papers also complement rather than compete with the photo.

Supplies: patterned paper, stickers, journaling card (Creative Imaginations); letters (Scenic Route); pen (EK Success)

EMBELLISHMENTS

An embellishment is anything you dress up your page with, such as letters, flowers and chipboard, button and brads, stickers and rub-ons, ribbon and trim. Buying and using embellishments are very much a part of the fun of scrapbooking. Coordinated product lines, which include embellishments that match the patterned paper, help you mix and match pieces with ease. When I find a product line I like, I buy as many coordinated products as possible!

Embellishments engage a reader when they support, rather than overwhelm, the photos. Begin with a title that drives a reader to take a closer look at the page. Choose different colors for letters or different fonts to emphasize your point. Continue to support your theme by using well-chosen papers and products. Be sure to leave white space; you don't want to clutter up your page with too many doodads.

Supplies: all products by KI Memories

ALPHABETS

If I could have a favorite product it would be letters—stickers, chipboard, rub-ons and anything else that I can use to make a title. The available textures include cardstock, foam, fabric and vinyl, and I love them all! Use letters to craft a title or design a stylish monogram for your layout.

My son Jacob used to sleep surrounded by his mix of colorful stuffed friends. Now they surround him in his room. I wanted to give this layout that same feel and did so by using a mix of leftover colorful letters for the title (a sample of some of the many types that are out there). The stacked sticker tags work as a single journaling block, while the two hand-cut photo corners add another splash of color.

Supplies: cardstock (Bazzill); labels (Scenic Route); letters (Doodlebug Designs, My Little Shoebox, American Crafts, KI Memories); pen (EK Success)

ACCENTS

Wondering what to do with all the white space surrounding your photos? Add a large silk flower, rub-on pattern, chipboard accent or sticker. Large accents provide texture and interest, but remember that a little goes a long way.

When designing with a single enlarged photo, use the photo as the foundation for all the page elements. Overlap the title onto the photo, use larger accents such as the chipboard letters and the hand-cut numerals used here, and layer these over the photo. The three journaling shapes all overlap each other and continue the connected property of the content.

Supplies: cardstock (Bazzill); letters (Maya Road); accents (K&Co.)

SMALL ACCENTS

Often a layout will need just a little something extra. When this is the case I turn to my small accents. You can use a brad or button to accent a larger embellishment, like the center of a flower, or use them on their own for infusing spots of color. I've found that these tiny products are addicting!

Leave white borders around your photos to make them stand out against a dark background. The themed embellishments here pop against the background and are enhanced by the hand-cut heart. The small embellishments that overlap parts of the layout connect the design.

Supplies: cardstock, labels, pen (American Crafts); letters (Prima Marketing); accents (Karen Foster); Misc: ribbon

It's sometimes difficult to get great photos of my husband and his father, so when I captured these beloved candids of the two of them, I knew I'd use them right away. I wanted to create a casual layout to reflect the mood of the photos. The torn strip of patterned paper with its curvy lines and the casually placed accents do just that. I used tiny brads to fasten the bookplate accent and larger brads grouped together as stand-alone embellishments. The fall-themed paper softens the overall look while keeping it masculine.

Supplies: cardstock (Bazzill); patterned paper (BasicGrey, Scenic Route); stickers (7Gypsies); brads (SEI); bookplate (Making Memories); pen (American Crafts)

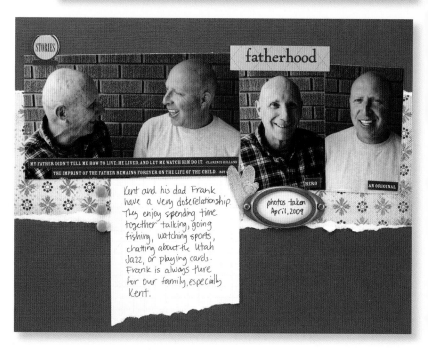

Embellish With Brads and Eyelets

What started out as boring office staples have grown into favorite scrapbook fasteners. Use single brads or eyelets to fasten trim or other embellishments, or line them up and have them stand on their own.

MATERIALS LIST
brads, paper piercer, foam or mat; eyelets, Crop-A-Dile

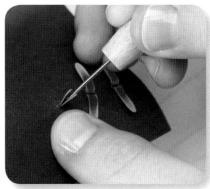

Lining up brads
To ensure brads are lined up and spaced properly, set them upside down next to where you want them to go. Then poke the holes with a paper piercer. Place a piece of foam, mat or a mouse pad under the paper before you pierce.

Opening tight prongs
Tight brad prongs can be tricky to open. Use a paper piercer to pry apart the prongs.

Setting eyelets
Eyelets work as well as brads for embellishing layouts. To easily insert an eyelet, use a Crop-A-Dile. First, punch a hole. Then insert the eyelet, and close it with the eyelet setting on the tool.

STAMPS

Stamps themselves aren't embellishments, but their result is certainly great for decorating a layout. Stamps allow you to create the same images over and over again. Alphabet stamps work for titles and monograms, while stamp shapes make great accents. And many companies produce stamps intended for creating space for journaling. You can choose from a variety of ink types, depending on your needs, but make sure they are scrapbook-safe products. Stamps are made from rubber or acrylic, and both materials have their benefits. Rubber is typically mounted on wood and transfers more intricate detail. Acrylic stamps have flooded the market. The transparent stamp image is typically separated from the stamping block; as long as you have a few blocks on hand, you need only purchase the images, making for easier storage. Another advantage of acrylic stamps is that they allow you to see exactly where you are placing an image on the page.

Remember **This**

Often, when people discover scrapbooking they fall in love with the products and start collecting them. Soon they are paralyzed by too much stuff and get frustrated every time they want to scrapbook. Avoid frustration by passing up items you do not have an immediate use for.

This layout's focus is on my son Nathan and how he is always a spot of light in his aunt's life. I used green patterned paper to create somewhat of a masculine feel and a floral print to contribute a feminine touch as well. The accents, while not all similar in color or shape, group together well to give a fun collage effect. Using the black rub-on in the embellishment cluster works well because the rub-on can go over a variety of surfaces like photo and paper.

Supplies: cardstock (DCWV); patterned paper (BasicGrey); rub-ons, button (Jenni Bowlin); letters (Pink Paislee)

Rub on Some Style

Turn to rub-ons when you want a splash of style or whimsy. Because they are thin and adhere well to photos, cardstock, paper or other accents, you can place them anywhere on a page or layer them over other elements to create depth. Attaching rub-ons can be tricky, but with the know-how you'll be a pro in no time.

MATERIALS LIST
rub-on, scissors, burnishing tool or craft stick

1. Cut out the rub-on you want to use. Trim closely around the design.

2. Peel away the backing.

3. Place the rub-on, sticky side (back side) down, in the desired location. Rub over the entire image completely with a craft stick or burnishing tool. As the rub-on is transferred, the sheet will begin to lift away.

4. Carefully lift away the sheet, checking to ensure that the entire image was transferred before removing completely.

TRIM AND RIBBON

Staples in sewing and quilting for years, ribbon and trim unsurprisingly began to show up in scrapbooking projects as well. Whether it's velvet ribbon, pom pom trim or simple rickrack, trim makes it easy to add a dash of texture and color.

This layout uses trim to ground and outline the photos and assorted papers, merging them into one connected block. The playful shape of the rickrack trim supports the child-friendly colors. In order to keep the eye moving around the entire layout, I added black ribbon to the top of the page to connect the title to the rest of the layout.

Supplies: cardstock (Prism); patterned paper, ribbon (American Crafts); letter stickers, brads (Doodlebug Designs)

Create Texture and Style With Trim

Adding trim to a layout gives it a handmade look, creating softness and texture. Add strips, bows, fringe or create your own tabs with ribbon—just make sure you have a strong adhesive that will hold it in place.

MATERIALS LIST
trim, scissors, adhesive strips (like Glue Lines)

1. Cut the trim to the desired length. (Note: Using sharp scissors will cut down on frayed ends. You may also want to apply a bit of liquid seam sealant to prevent fraying, or tuck the ends of the trim behind the background paper to hide them.)

2. Cut a length of adhesive strip to about the same length as the ribbon. Press the trim to the adhesive strip and smooth with your fingertips to affix securely.

3. Remove the backing from the adhesive strip. Position the trim along the edges between two papers and/or photos and press down on the layout to adhere.

4. Cut a second smaller length of trim. Add a small piece of adhesive strip to the front and back of the layout. Fold the trim in half and attach to create a tab.

Albums

With all of the layouts you'll be making, you need to select a quality album to house them. Albums differ in their binding and the materials they are made of. First, determine what type of binding you want, and then find an album that suits your style.

POST-BOUND

You can expand the width of post-bound albums by adding more pages and post extenders. When assembled, the layouts are flush with each other.

THREE-RING

Constructed similarly to everyday notebook binders, three-ring albums are my favorite type in which to store my layouts. The rings make it simple to insert and remove pages, plus the large spine allows for lots of layouts.

STRAP-HINGE

Strap-hinge albums are bound with a plastic strap that connects the covers and pages through a staple on the page binding. Closing the binding can be tricky at first, as you want the straps tight to ensure a good album fit. You then use a side-load page protector that slips over the layout. The nice aspect of the strap-hinge is that due to the side-loading protector, it is much more difficult for dust to get onto your layouts. The disadvantage is that to add more pages you need to undo the entire binding and insert the page exactly where you want it to go.

POST-BOUND ALBUM

THREE-RING ALBUM

Your Scrap Space

So now that you have all the tools and materials at your disposal, where are you going to put them? Having a dedicated scrap space—even if it's just a portable box at the coffee table or the corner of the dining room—will help you stay motivated and make time. And keeping your space organized is essential for successful scrapbooking and keeping your sanity.

SETTING UP YOUR WORK SPACE

When determining your scrap space location, consider your preferences while working. For example, do you prefer to be in the mix of everything while working, or do you need a quiet space? If you have the luxury of setting up a dedicated scrap space, start by making sure everything has a place: Keep what you use the most closest to you and store everything else in dedicated shelves and containers. Also select an adequate work surface, one that is large enough to spread out and at the right height (for standing or sitting). Once you have an idea of where you will create, use that information to dictate the type of storage you need. If you are going to scrapbook mainly on the go, invest in a wheeled scrapbook tote and storage boxes for your pages in progress. If you are creating in a shared space, keep your supplies to a minimum.

STORING MATERIALS

First you need to know what you are storing, then you need to know where it is going: behind closet doors, on an open shelf, in a portable file, etc. Baskets can hold bulky items like punches and stamps. Paper files are a great solution for organizing patterned paper and sheets of accents. Binders are also a good solution for storing sheets. Set up glass jars for storing ribbon and small accents, and sort them by color. Save drawers for items like paint and adhesive.

Tool Kit Worksheet

Before you go out and purchase the local scrapbooking store's entire supply of goods, think about what you already have and what's essential to buy right now.

Tools + Materials I Have	Tools + Materials I Need to Start	Dream Tools + Materials
_____	_____	_____
_____	_____	_____
_____	_____	_____
_____	_____	_____
_____	_____	_____
_____	_____	_____
_____	_____	_____

Chapter Three

Telling the Story

Scrapbooking is popularly known as a way to display or decorate photos. While that is true, it is also a powerful means of communicating. Part of the process of preserving memories in scrapbooks is to share the stories behind the moments. Two main elements contribute to the storytelling process: photos and words (and memorabilia plays a part as well). Different layouts will require different approaches to storytelling; some may play up the words while others will focus on the photos. And within each approach there are multiple ways to highlight the story. Regardless of how you choose to use photos and words together, your precious stories are sure to emerge.

Telling the Story With Photos

We've all heard the saying, a photo is worth a thousand words. For scrapbookers, however, it has to be the right photo. As you look over your photos, you may find that you didn't shoot exactly what you wanted in order to tell a particular story. The perspective of a scrapbooker is different than a nonscrapbooker, so the content needs of your photos will change. With this, you'll begin to look for opportunities to capture life in different ways. Be thinking about the stories you want to tell, and look for ways the photos you take can assist you.

As you start looking through the camera lens as a scrapbooker, you will find images that you want to photograph that will enhance your storytelling. The sign photos on this layout are a perfect example. You don't see a subject in these images; they are strictly informative. But that is why I shot them. I wanted to remember the names and locations of the campgrounds we stayed at on vacation.

Supplies: cardstock (Bazzill); patterned paper (Rusty Pickle); wood signs (Karen Foster); Misc: Nyala font

Tips for Taking Better Photos

- **Get closer to your subject.** Fill the frame with your subject.
- **Vary the angle.** Try shooting your subject from above, below or even the side. Different angles make layouts interesting.
- **Catch the rays.** Learn where to place your subjects in relation to the sun.
- **Take lots and lots of photos.** The more you take, the better your chances are for getting a remarkable image.
- **Read your camera's manual.** Studying what your camera can do and practicing with it will help you improve exponentially.

I am usually the one taking the photos, so when Kent offered to take the photos I eagerly handed over the camera. Five things that make me happy when I remember this photo being taken are listed below.
1. being outside in the sun
2. spending time with family
3. getting Ben's cookies after
4. talking to Kent
5. listening to the kids play.

why I am **smiling**

To get this photograph, I handed over the camera to my husband, Kent, and asked him to be the photographer for the day. He enjoys taking photos of the kids from time to time and always tries to get a few shots of me. Next time you are wandering around with the camera, hand it over, and get in the picture for a change.

Supplies: patterned paper (BasicGrey, My Mind's Eye); journaling card (Jenni Bowlin); letters (Pink Paislee, Doodlebug Designs); circle accent (Prima Marketing); pen (EK Success)

Quick Tip

It's common for the one who takes the family photos to be excluded from a majority of the photographs. Avoid that by handing over the camera to someone else or utilizing your camera's timer. You'll be glad you did because you'll have proof you existed and participated in the many outings and special events!

Photographing pets is no easy task, which is why I handed the camera to my son, Justin. Our family cat, Pepper, selected Justin as her favorite the minute we brought her home as a kitten. She has since been with us twelve years and continues to prefer Justin's company. The journaling is a poem Justin wrote in a junior high English class.

Supplies: cardstock (Bazzill); patterned paper (Doodlebug Designs); letters (Heidi Swapp); Misc: Cheapprofontsserif font

---

Even if your photo-taking is less than stellar, you can use photos to tell the story. An eye-catching design and smaller photos will distract from the flaws. Give your pages high impact by leaving generous amounts of empty space around the photos. Extend the graphic feel by using just one or two colors in combination with a few small black-and-white photographs. Bleed part of your title off the edge of your page as Cathy did on this layout.

Supplies: cardstock (Bazzill); die-cut letters and punctuation (QuicKutz); Misc: Interstate font

Artwork by *Cathy Zielske*

Clean clothes or a hot meal on the table? Hot meal, or quality time? Quality time or meeting deadlines? Meeting deadlines or clean clothes? I'm finding it really hard to strike a deal with balance. I have this finite number of hours each day. A good chunk is already lost to sleep, and how I'm balancing the remaining 17 is anyone's guess. I love my family. My friends. What I do for a living. When my house is clean. When kids are ably cared for. Occasionally, the bill is too tall to fill on all accounts. I wish to be stellar and succeed in all areas, but I'm thinking there's one insurmountable obstacle: I'm human. I think it's all about mastering transitions: when one load is complete, you put in another. Then, you move on. The problem is, I always come back to the load to check on it, over and over and over. So much for life as laundry metaphors. I need to find a way to keep the scales more even.

{BALANCE}

Photo Organization

Is it even possible to organize all your photos? Yes it is! You need to (a) set up a system so you can access photos, and (b) actually use that system. Organizing printed photos and digital photo files is a complex task, and one that shouldn't be completed overnight (if you want to keep your sanity). Break down the task into manageable chunks, and once everything you have is organized, be sure to maintain the organization. Doing a little every day or week will save you loads of time in the long run and help you see exactly what photos you have to tell your story.

PRINT PHOTO ORGANIZATION

Before you start a task, I recommend setting a realistic goal for yourself and creating a task list. Gather all photos and negatives. Determine your goal(s): Are you digitizing photos? Are you making copies for family members? What is your budget? How much time can you dedicate? After you have figured out what you are doing with the photos, you are ready to start organizing. The following steps are a suggestion of how to proceed, but feel free to delete or add steps you see necessary.

1. Sort photos into categories (e.g., month/year, person or event)

2. Label the back of each photo with the category (using an archival marking pen)

3. Digitize each photo (if this is part of your plan)

4. Store prints in archival containers, organized by category (if you are keeping photos)

As for where to store all those photos, archival storage boxes are great for holding a massive collection; each box holds about one-thousand prints. Photo envelopes are meant for long-term storage, but are also handy for portable scrapbooking. Photo print binders are useful when you want to easily flip through a collection and move prints around.

Quick Tip

My favorite online resources for photo safe, archival storage are www.lineco.com and archivalmethods.com.

DIGITAL PHOTO ORGANIZATION

A few questions to ask yourself as you determine how to proceed: How do you prefer to access the images? By file name? By tags? Do you plan on storing all your digital files on your computer? Do you have a digital backup? What type of files do you want to save your images in? How are you going to organize the files: by date, person, event or some of both? Once you've determined the best categorization for your photos, create folders on your computer's hard drive in which you'll store the photos. (Instead, you can install a program such as Picasa [http://picasa.google.com] to help you organize photos.) You'll want to create and label a few main folders (such as for the year or family members) and several subfolders (such as the month or activity). Then spend some time organizing the photos already on your hard drive (and uploading any photos still on your memory card). Once old photos are organized, you can start the task of organizing new photos as you take them. Below is the process I use, but feel free to adapt any or all of it to fit your needs. If you take photos daily, I recommend uploading photos from your camera to your computer weekly so it's easier to keep photos organized as you go.

1. Upload photos to computer.

2. Create new folders as needed and sort photos into the appropriate folder. Label photos.

3. Delete unwanted photos.

4. If you're using organization software, add applicable tags to photos (such as person's name or subject).

5. Make a physical backup (either by burning a CD, moving to a backup drive or uploading to a photo storage site; I pay a small amount each month for Google to host my images).

6. Order prints or print photos on an at-home printer.

Photo Output

In today's digital world, the creative things you can do with your photos are seemingly endless—everything from altering them digitally to turning them into a puzzle to printing them the size of a poster. Printing standard-sized photos (whether you use them whole or crop them) makes output simple, so you will find yourself working mostly with standard-sized prints. But occasionally you'll want to try enlargements (like 8" × 10" [20cm × 25cm] or smaller prints to spice things up.

Prior to output, consider editing your photos, taking time to make them black and white, crop, remove red eye or resize them. To determine which editing program you should use, figure out what you want to do with your images. If you want to make quick fixes like cropping and fixing red eye, a free program such as Picasa will do the job. If you want to resize photos, adjust curves, change the lighting or whiten teeth, for example, you are better off with a more extensive image-editing software program such as Adobe Photoshop Elements, which is popular with many scrapbookers.

Photo-editing software allows you to resize your photos and create cute mini prints as Celeste did for this layout. You can even add a digital white border to photos to save the paper and time you would use matting images. Placing the photos, title and accents on the same line keeps the page design simple and fresh. Type or write your journaling on white and justify to the right, balancing your page with the large shape on the left and different patterns on the page.

Supplies: cardstock (Bazzill); patterned paper, stickers, die-cuts, stamp (October Afternoon); tab punch (McGill); Misc: buttons, Another Typewriter font

Artwork by *Celeste Smith*

USING ENLARGEMENTS

When ordinary images are magnified, the visual experience changes. Using enlargements can give a page an interesting and bold effect. Keep in mind that making a photo larger will make any flaw more obvious, so enlarge just the best photos. Scrapbook the enlargements the same way you would standard-sized photos, though you'll need to stick to fewer images on the page. Large photos you already have stashed away, like family portraits and class photos, are a good opportunity to try out using enlargements on a layout.

{ you rock }

You'd been itching for it. You know, really hinting around how nice it would be to have one. Enter one sucker (that would be me) for a kid who needs to rock and a short trip to Guitar Center. If you never take a lesson a day in your life, it wouldn't matter. I think you're the coolest kid ever. G chord, or no G chord. Coley, you rock.

JULY 2006

Enlarge a black-and-white photo to use as a background for your page. Doing so provides a great focal point upon which the eye can rest, and it reemphasizes the theme of your layout. Print your main photo in color to lend an interesting contrast. Finish off your design with a few simple embellishments like the brads along the bottom edge of Cathy's layout.

Supplies: cardstock (Bazzill); brads (KI Memories); Misc: adhesive foam, Interstate font

Artwork by *Cathy Zielske*

Photo Printers: Best Buys

A great tool to have in your scrap space is a personal photo printer, so you can print photos from your hard drive on demand. Many also allow you to insert your memory card and print photos instantly. Ideal for printing a handful of photos at a time, these printers are generally under $200. My personal pick is the Epson PictureMate line, but the Canon Selphy and HP Photosmart printers are also great buys.

PHOTO RESTORATION

When word gets around that you are scrapbooking, you might find yourself inheriting all of the family photos. If you do get the opportunity and responsibility to catalog and preserve old photos, you'll need some help, whether it's the aid of image-editing software or professional photo restoration services. Using scans of original photos, image-editing software such as Photoshop Elements can do wonders to remove tears and scratches, discoloration and other flaws of age. Alternatively, hiring professional help will ensure scans are restored brilliantly, and many services can restore originals as well. Regardless of how you restore vintage photos, be sure to include them in your albums—these photos provide a rich source for stories.

When working with vintage images, select accompanying products wisely. Avoid bright colors and trendy patterns, and instead use classic designs and supporting patterns similar to the ones I used here. Quiet designs keep the focus on the photos, which can easily get lost considering pictures' subtle tones. In addition, today's trendy products often look garish next to refined older photographs. To complement this black-and-white photo, I selected darker colored patterned paper and used a vintage typewriter font.

Supplies: patterned paper (KI Memories, Graphic 45); stickers (Making Memories); Misc: Traveling typewriter font, tag

Digitizing Photos and Negatives

DO IT YOURSELF
You can digitize photos yourself with a computer and scanner equipped to scan negatives, slides and/or photographs. Scanners like the Epson Perfection and Canon Canoscan include a built-in transparency unit that allows you to easily scan slides and negatives.

While it would feel great to have everything digitized at once, it isn't a small task to complete, so give yourself permission to work bit by bit, as time allows. The important thing is to remember that you are making a good effort to take care of your memories.

SEND IT OUT
To save yourself time, use a service like Larsen Digital (www.slidescanning.com) or ScanCafe (www.scancafe.com), which will send scan and organize photos for you.

Telling the Story With Words

The most significant aspect of telling the story with words involves journaling—the part of a layout in which you tell the details of the story. Journaling can range from listing a few basic facts to typing multiple paragraphs. Not everyone is a natural with words, so journaling can be the biggest challenge for many. As you tackle this part of scrapbooking consider who will read it. Why are you sharing this story? What is important to document with words? Good writing takes practice; however, your personality and voice will come through as long as you keep it real.

You don't have to write a book to tell the story of a photo in words. On this layout, I just wrote a sentence about the photo—the smiles tell the rest of the story. If you don't have much to say, try journaling in the empty space around your photo. This will avoid cluttering your page with an extra design element.

Supplies: patterned paper (Chatterbox); letters (American Crafts); stickers (Chatterbox)

Tips for Meaningful Journaling

- **Be yourself.** You are telling the story from your perspective, so use your own voice and write the same way you talk.

- **Step outside yourself.** Think of what you would want to know about the photos if you were someone else. Who is in them and why? Where is the photo taken? Why it is important to photograph and scrapbook? Asking yourself these questions will provide a starting point.

- **Describe the details.** Include information about the sounds, the sights, the feeling. Be specific because this is what makes your story uniquely your own.

- **Change it up.** Try different approaches like using quotations or making lists. This will make journaling more enjoyable to write and more interesting to read.

- **Read to become a better writer.** From fiction to nonfiction, reading will give you context for good writing, which will help you with your journaling.

Approaches to Journaling

Understanding the different approaches to journaling will enable you to choose the most meaningful and effective way to share your words on a page. And different pages will require different approaches. Using various methods helps you keep journaling from becoming monotonous (for you and the reader) and allows you to focus on different parts of memories.

TELL A STORY

Sharing the complete story usually entails recounting the details of a particular event or experience in a chronological manner. This type of journaling includes specific details and the storyteller's perspective of the events. Use this approach for layouts that cover topics such as how you met your partner, why you changed jobs, how it felt to become a mother or your child's favorite birthday gift.

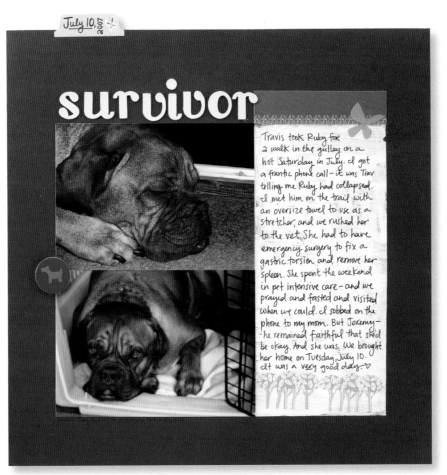

On this layout, Angie relates the story of her dog's medical scare; the photos support the details of the story. Angie uses a lot of handwritten text set in a long column, which helps with readability. Working with rich jewel tones, Angie needed a way to set apart the journaling. She did so by painting a simple rectangle and journaling on the dried paint with her favorite black pen. This makes the journaling pop off the page.

Supplies: cardstock (Prism); letters (American Crafts); accents (SEI); Misc: acrylic paint

Artwork by *Angie Lucas*

GIVE 'EM JUST THE FACTS

Some topics don't demand a long story. Choose to list the essential facts and throw in a few details to make it more lively. Think about what details you will want to recall over the years to guide yourself in determining what content to include.

Journaling in bits and pieces of text, as I did here, works well when you're journaling just the main parts of the story. Because of the busy nature of the photos on this layout, I kept the background plain and simple. I used photo corners to group photos together, allowing them to tell a story. Don't be afraid to break up a title as long as it flows naturally across the page.

Supplies: patterned paper (American Crafts); letters (American Crafts, Making Memories); brads (Doodlebug Designs); Misc: Eurofurence font

Create Journaling Strips

Regardless of whether you handwrite or type words, slicing journaling into strips creates nice, clean lines that enhance the design of a simple page. Plus, strips break up the text to add visual interest.

MATERIALS LIST
cardstock with printed or handwritten journaling (triple-spaced), paper trimmer or scissors, adhesive, brads

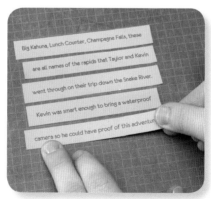

1. Trim rows of text using a paper trimmer or scissors. Leave at least ½" (13mm) of empty space at the beginning of each strip. You may choose to keep all the strips the same length or vary the lengths for a more casual look.

2. Adhere strips to the page, leaving a bit of space between each row.

3. Poke a hole at the beginning of each row, and insert a small brad.

MAKE A LIST

Lists are easy to write and quick to finish, and they make wonderful additions to layouts. You can make lists for all kinds of topics, like holiday gifts, ingredients for a favorite recipe, highlights from the month, New Year's resolutions and favorite books.

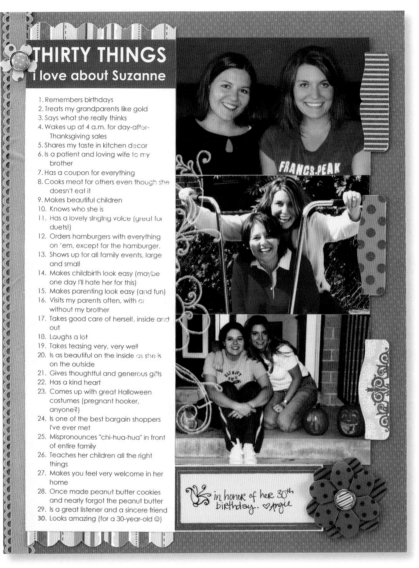

This layout features both specific characteristics and events that comprise the list of things Angie loves about her sister-in-law. Angie has an album that houses layouts for members of her family that lists thirty things she loves about each of them. Consider listing what you love about family members, hobbies, your home, places you visit or family traditions.

Supplies: patterned paper, stickers, flowers, brads (Making Memories)

Artwork by *Angie Lucas*

USE THE "WRITE" STUFF

Think of all the written communication you are involved with daily, from blog posts to birthday cards to quick notes left on a pad of self-adhesive paper. These are key parts of your life and they are rich with journaling content. Next time you need words for journaling, consider using the handwritten note you left in your son's lunch box or the funny birthday greeting your sister sent you.

As a blogger, I have found ideas for journaling in many entries, especially those about family members or daily life. On my blog, I listed some of my husband's traits in recognition of an upcoming anniversary and later used the post as journaling on this page. I found a recent photo and paired it with the journaling to create a quick and meaningful layout about a very important person in my life.

Supplies: cardstock (American Crafts); patterned paper (BasicGrey); brads (Making Memories) Misc: 28 Days Later and Cicle fonts

Quick Tip

One of my favorite journaling products are those journaling blocks bound in notebooks. You can carry them in your purse, journal on the go, then adhere to a layout later.

RECORD THE STATS

Stats can communicate much information in few words. (Just think of all that sports fans can glean from reading the stats from the latest sporting game.) Of course, you can use this approach for sports-themed layouts, but stats also make sense when you're recording a child's school information, hobbies, extra curricular activities and more.

stats

league – mini metro

team – Colchester champs

season – winter 2008/2009

position – forward

height – 5' 3.5"

shoe size – 9 ½

Try using stats as journaling points in a sports-themed layout. Stats such as team, season, position and size are all you need to tell an effective story. Using a bright color scheme and circles on a sports layout conveys action and excitement.

Supplies: patterned paper (Scenic Route); letter stickers (American Crafts); star die-cuts (QuicKutz)

Artwork by *Katrina Simeck*

JOT IT DOWN

If you think like I do, you don't think in complete sentences. So why not journal they way you think? This approach is one of my favorites because it is easy to execute and applicable to any subject. All you have to do is jot down your thoughts on a subject and add them to a layout. You can write your thoughts in an orderly fashion, such as a bulleted list, or in a more free-flowing, stream-of-consciousness style. To jump-start this kind of journaling, start with a general statement, such as "lessons learned from my little brother," and jot down everything you can think of.

A clever technique for jotting down thoughts on a page is to use brads as bullet points. You can write your thoughts in a list form, as I did here, or insert brads between thoughts in a paragraph. This gives you an opportunity to say a lot but keep the design clean. Use up your stash of scrap paper to accent a photo and title to continue the clean design.

Supplies: cardstock (DCWV); patterned paper (Adornit); decorative tape (Prima Marketing); letters, brads, chipboard accent (American Crafts)

Quick Tip

Thoughts come to you no matter where you are, so be prepared by keeping a notebook handy at all times to jot down notes for journaling.

DO SOME EAVESDROPPING

Snippets of conversations can be revealing and fun to preserve as journaling on your layouts. Using this approach allows you to include others' perspectives in your albums. Write down conservations or intriguing quotations you hear, and then pair them with engaging photos of the subject(s). These kinds of layouts help readers feel like they are in on the conversation.

Reading the comments Lain's daughter Calli made, you get a sense of her upbeat and funny personality. The quirky painted background supports the quirky quotes. The engaging photos and patterned paper border anchor the layout and provide visual context to the journaling.

Supplies: cardstock (Bazzill); patterned paper (K&Co.); letters (Mustard Moon, Karen Foster); pen (American Crafts); Misc: acrylic paint

Artwork by *Lain Ehmann*

Remember This

No one expects you to write like a professional, so let your own voice out. It's okay to write like you talk (in other words, not proper sentences). Remember who is going to be reading your words—your loved ones and you. They'll love you no matter what, so allow yourself the freedom to just write.

SHARE THE HIGHLIGHTS

When we relate stories to one another, what we often do is merely share the highlights. Try incorporating this approach with your journaling. Have you returned from a vacation with hundreds of photos? Pick your top ten and express the reasons they are your top choice—journaling done!

As a generation that takes hundreds of photos of a single event, our photo selections can be unbearable. This page features nine photos from the last few years of my son Jacob's life with journaling that shares different parts of his personality and his interests. This approach illustrates growth physically and emotionally. Consider it for personality pages, building a new home, baby's first year or anything that changes over time.

Supplies: cardstock (Bazzill); patterned paper (BasicGrey); letters (Doodlebug Design); numbers (My Little Shoebox); pen (American Crafts)

REMEMBER THIS

You know how you think you will never, ever forget certain events or people in your life? At the time you create a layout it may seem unnecessary and silly to note the day, place or people in a photo. But you'll thank yourself later for including these details that you can no longer recall. Use brief captions to record the necessities so you never find yourself muttering, "Um, who is that?"

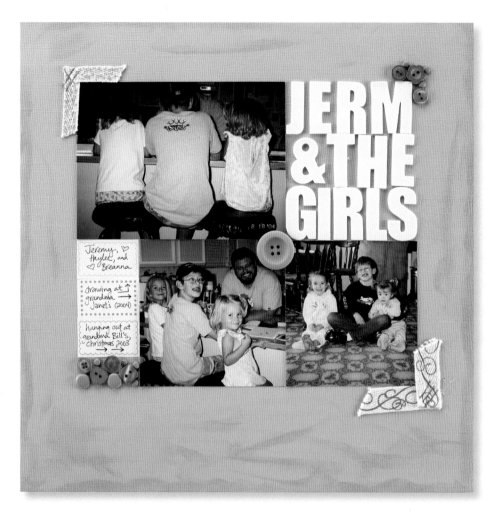

Some of my favorite photos are shot from behind. I like them because it gives me a unique look at what is going on between subjects. But backside photos can make it tricky to recall names or dates down the road. On this layout, you can see one such photo in the top right where both girls are nestled right next to Jeremy. Angie composed brief captions for this layout so she can recall the events years from now.

Supplies: patterned paper, ribbon (Autumn Leaves); letters (American Crafts); Misc: buttons, brads

Artwork by *Angie Lucas*

Journaling Styles

Handwritten and typed journaling are both appropriate styles for layouts. You'll probably find yourself preferring one style over the other, but it's important to mix it up every now and then to keep pages fresh.

SIGN HERE, PLEASE

It is important to use your handwriting at least once in a while in your scrapbooks even if you don't care for your handwriting. Think about it: When you see your child's handwriting you probably experience an emotional reaction. Or when you see your grandparents' handwriting you feel nostalgic. I look at handwritten recipes of my mom's and I immediately think about the comforts of home, not "man, my mom's handwriting is not so cute." So use your handwriting every now and then.

This is a rare photo of my mom and her older sister, my Aunt Virgie. Growing up my mom lived with her parents and her four siblings in a dumpy shack with dirt floors. This photo is taken in their front yard. They were always very poor and were looked down on by the townspeople. My mom is a strong woman because of her upbringing. She has dedicated much of her life to giving to others of her time and talents. I am proud of what she has done with what she was given.

I used vintage patterned paper to coordinate with the old black-and-white photo, and used a crocheted flower to enhance the cozy, old-fashioned feel. Telling the story with handwriting furthers the homespun feeling. The ornate rub-on border on the photo mat grounds that element, while the neutral-colored background really allows the photo and journaling to shine.

Supplies: cardstock (Prism); patterned paper (Graphic 45); flower (Fancy Pants); rub-on (Melissa Frances); pen (American Crafts)

Personalize With Your Handwriting

Handwritten journaling adds personality to a layout. Plus, it is much less complicated to write on your layouts than to add type to them. If you're concerned about the sloppiness of your writing or making spelling mistakes, following a few simple steps will help you on your way to handwriting with ease.

MATERIALS LIST
clear ruler, pencil, journaling pen, art gum eraser

1. Use a clear ruler and pencil to lightly draw pencil lines for journaling. Using a clear ruler gives you a better view to keep the spacing of the lines just right.

2. Compose your journaling in pencil, using the lines to guide you, making any corrections along the way.

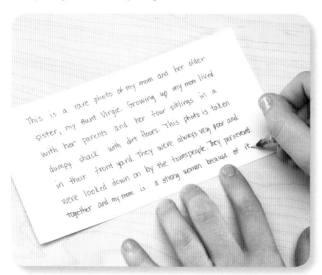

3. Trace over the penciled journaling with a journaling pen. Allow the ink to dry.

4. Gently erase the pencil lines using a art gum eraser (to avoid marking your paper).

Variation
You can also use this technique to easily create curved or wavy lines of journaling.

JUST YOUR TYPE

It's only nautral to want to type the words on our layouts. Computer-generated journaling is readable, and you can fit longer stories by using smaller text. You can construct text boxes and graphics, not to mention download lots of fun fonts. Keep font sizes no smaller than about 10 points for maximum readability.

Soft, feminine colors can be used on a layout about a young man when the journaling is from a feminine perspective, such as a mother about a son. On this layout, simple strips of patterned paper add color and balance the masculine subject. The quirky, puffy stickers inject playfulness. One photo is all it takes to illustrate the journaling, which is computer generated. As you can see, computer-generated journaling allows for lots of text to fit on a page. Keep in mind that typed text is easier to read when positioned with 1½ spaces between lines.

Supplies: patterned paper (Pink Paislee, My Mind's Eye); stickers (American Crafts); Misc: Rhino Dino and David fonts

Triadic color schemes are perfect for illustrating cheerfulness without overpowering a design. Fun fonts also do the trick. The playful bold font enforces the story of the layout, and by printing it in a primary color it becomes kid-friendly. Embellishments such as rickrack and a wavy paper border enhance the overall liveliness. Use the same color for the letters and a fun journaling font to polish off your own design.

Supplies: cardstock (Bazzill); paper trim (Sassafras Lass); brads, sticker (American Crafts); Misc: Cheri font

Free Fonts

The Web abounds with sources for free fonts. Check out these sites to find new favorites:

- www.twopeasinabucket.com/freefonts.asp
- www.dafont.com
- www.scrapvillage.com/fonts.htm

Today's Headlines

Titles are also part of sharing your story with words. When working on a title, think of newspaper headlines that catch your eye—this is what you want your title to do. A good title immediately connects the photo to the layout's theme and hints at the journaling, and it draws the reader into the layout. Titles make for fun design elements as well.

One signature of city life is all of the different signs surrounding the area. I was fascinated with the polite and descriptive nature of the signs flooding the streets of Sydney, Australia, and thoroughly enjoyed photographing them. The page title speaks to the page theme and a strong memory of my visit. It also works to grab attention and provide a cohesiveness to the collage of photographs.

Supplies: cardstock (Bazzill); patterned paper (October Afternoon); Misc: Bebas font

As I mentioned, alphabet products are my favorites, and the ones used on this layout are no exception. The direction and placement of this title were starting points for the page. The title immediately draws readers into the journaling, which leads to an understanding of the photo and the theme. Bright and colorful, just like the T-shirt in the photos, this layout shares a favorite family tradition.

Supplies: cardstock (DCWV); patterned paper (Scenic Route); letters (American Crafts); brads (Bazzill)

Telling the Story With Memorabilia

Making memorabilia a part of your layouts is probably a familiar idea to you—historically, scrapbooks have included memorabilia. It is only recently that we have forgone the practice in favor of fancy products. Including memorabilia on a layout adds an extra layer of information to a project; memorabilia gives context to the photos. Plus, it is a visual representation of a time or event, which is important to include in albums.

Winning the Pinewood Derby was a first for someone in our family, and Caden was filled with pride as he collected his first-place ribbon. The original ribbon hangs on a shelf in his bedroom for all to see. I wanted to include it on this layout and to do so, I made a color copy of it. To make the copy look authentic, I added trim and a dimensional embellishment.

Supplies: cardstock (Bazzill); letters, brads (Doodlebug Designs); numbers (Karen Foster); stickers (K&Co.); pen (EK Success)

Five Reasons to Include Memorabilia

1. **To complete the story.** Look at the latest concert ticket stub in your possession (or something similar): All the details are listed, from date to location to time.

2. **To add style.** Memorabilia often has an interesting design.

3. **To further illustrate the story.** For example, a map can show the distance you traveled during a road trip.

4. **To serve as a time capsule of your everyday life.**

5. **To help you remember the little details of life.** Record a busy football schedule or how much the food on your fantastic vacation cost.

Including Memorabilia Safely

Unlike products made for scrapbooking, memorabilia is not typically photo safe, meaning it may damage your photos over time. The acid in paper memorabilia will vary as much as the types of memorabilia. To be on the safe side, only include memorabilia that has been treated or copied.

DEACIDIFYING

If you want to include paper memorabilia, treat it with a deacidification spray such as Archival Mist (shown at left). This spray will neutralize acid in just about any paper item, like newspaper clippings and children's artwork.

SCANNING AND COPYING

Copying or scanning original memorabilia (onto acid-free pape, of course!) and including the printed version will protect a layout. This also gives you flexibility in your design because you can resize the memorabilia as needed.

On this layout, I included the tags from the clothes that my son and I bought from a day at the mall. The design of the clothing tags gives this layout a look that mirrors that of the clothing shown in the photos. Plus, it provides a glimpse into the style and design of the times, which will be fun to remember years down the road.

Supplies: cardstock (Bazzill); patterned paper (Sassafras Lass); letters (American Crafts); Misc: notebook paper, tags

Since I wanted to preserve all the memorabilia from my trip of a lifetime to New Zealand, I devised this pocket to hold my treasures. I used foam adhesive to make the pocket extra roomy, and I used coordinating products to whip everything together in a snap. The pocket allows me to display and preserve everything from my trip and still access the memorabilia if I want to use it in other projects. Use this technique for birthday cards, Valentines, menus, travel maps and more.

Supplies: patterned paper (BasicGrey, Making Memories); letters (My Little Shoebox, BasicGrey); die-cut letters (QuicKutz)

Craft an Easy Memorabilia Pocket

When you have a lot of memorabilia you want to condense onto one layout, place it in a pocket page. These are quick and easy to make and can hold more memorabilia than a regular layout can.

MATERIALS LIST
patterned paper, paper trimmer, foam adhesive

1. For a 12" x 12" [30cm x 30cm] layout, cut one piece of patterned paper to 11½" × 4½" (29cm x 11cm). This will be the pocket. Cut a strip of coordinating patterned paper the same length and about 1" (3cm) wide. Set this piece aside.

2. On the back of the pocket, apply foam adhesive to the bottom and two sides.

3. Affix the pocket to the bottom half of the background paper. Attach the strip of paper over the top of the pocket along the top edge.

65

Don't Forget the Kids

There is something special about children's artwork. Maybe because it's so innocent, and children are unafraid to share their little creations. Consider using art as the photo, journaling or embellishment on a layout.

Have you found a special note drawn by a child? These hand-drawn bits are ordinary today, but won't last forever, thus making a great accessory to a layout. Elizabeth's layout features a handwritten note from the older sister to the younger sister stating her love. Scaled to fit this page, it reinforces the young age of the girls and the way they feel about each other.

Supplies: cardstock (Bazzill); letters (American Crafts); butterfly stamp (100 Proof Press); Misc: ink

Artwork by *Elizabeth Dillow*

Children's artwork represents the carefree part of our worlds. Including it on a layout serves to freeze time and to highlight the value placed on the art piece. This Valentine layout is an example of how Paula felt when she received a handmade love note from her son. To enhance the memory, she photographed the little artist holding the love note so she can remember how big the note was compared to her little boy.

Supplies: cardstock (Bazzill); letters (Li'l Davis Designs, Heidi Swapp); journaling tag (Adornit); floss (Karen Foster); Misc: fabric, ribbon, buttons

Artwork by *Paula Girarade*

Storing Memorabilia

If you're going to use memorabilia on your scrapbook layouts, it is important to be able to access those saved bits of information. You can organize these many different ways, but the best way will be the one that works for you. I suggest storing the memorabilia in a archival box and tagging them in the same way you do your photos, so you can easily match photos and memorabilia when it's time to scrap them. You can also store your memorabilia with your printed photos, placing your treated memorabilia in page protectors right next to the prints. That way, when it is time to scrapbook, everything will be in the same place.

Quick Tip

Using divided page protectors to contain your memorabilia and extra photos is a great alternative to scrapbooking all of it. You can find divided page protectors at your local scrapbook store, camera store or craft store.

Storytelling Planner

Use this worksheet to help you plan how you will tell your stories. This will save you time (you can get right down to creating!) and also allow you to record your thoughts while they're on your mind and save them for scrapbooking later. Start the sheet with the part of the story you have to tell (the photo, words or memorabilia).

Topic to scrap: _____

Photo(s) to include: _____
    Preparation required (e.g., restoring, printing, enlarging): _____

Words to include: _____
_____
_____
_____

    Journaling approach: _____
    Journaling style: _____
    Possible titles: _____

Memorabilia to include: _____
    Preparation required (e.g., treating, copying): _____

Chapter Four

Designing a Layout

Now that you understand the different storytelling components of a layout, it's time to put it all together. This is the fun part! Getting started can often be a challenge, so I'll show you how to begin a page design from various starting points.

Why does any layout design work? Is it the colors of the products? The captions? The photographs? It's never just one element, but rather all of the elements working together, that makes a layout brilliant or blah. Though style is subjective, certain elements need to be in place for a layout to be successful. In this chapter, I'll introduce and explain basic design principles to ensure you create an attractive page every time.

Starting Points

A common misconception is that scrapbooking is simple enough that everyone approaches it basically the same way. I mean, how many different approaches can there be when we're just talking about photos, paper and words, right? Wrong! There are many different ways to build a layout and with multiple starting points. Keep in mind that you might prefer different processes for different layout goals. My process changes from time to time depending on what I'm trying to accomplish and what I have to start with.

The goal with any scrapbook page is to combine separate elements into a cohesive whole. This layout started with bright, cheery photos, but I used colorful patterned papers to enhance the asymmetrical design. The successful design pulls everything together to communicate the story, which is about an energetic and playful relationship between these two silly kids.

Supplies: patterned paper, trim (Sassafras Lass); letters (KI Memories); jewels (KaiserCraft); pen (American Crafts)

START WITH PHOTOS

Most scrappers choose the photos for a layout first. This is a logical place to begin because, after all, photos are the foundation of scrapbooking. But with the mass of photos to choose from, even starting with a photo can be daunting. Which ones do you choose? When you're browsing through computer files or boxes of pictures, your brain will naturally scan for connections. Often it will be obvious that certain photos go together—photos that were taken at the same event or location, for example. But encourage yourself to look for other connections too, like photos taken from a similar vantage point (for instance, from behind as loved ones walk toward a new adventure), or pictures that show the same inherited physical trait in different people. Open your mind and look beyond the obvious, and you'll enhance your ability to tell meaningful stories with photos.

FIRST DAY of

FOURTH grade

Caden tried his best to hide his excitment on the first day of school. he didn't fool me as he skipped along to school. 8/09

The focus of this layout is my son Caden's different nonverbal communications as he anticipates his first day at school. His expression is both excited and tentative. I started this layout by choosing photos that spoke to me, and the design took off from there. I selected products that matched the colors in the photos (Caden's backpack), and I emphasized the importance of my photos by keeping design, techniques and products very minimal. Here, my photos take center stage.

Supplies: patterned paper (Daisy D's); letters (Luxe Designs, American Crafts); journaling sticker (American Crafts); pen (Sakura)

Remember This

After you have been scrapbooking for a while, you'll find yourself taking photos more intentionally, in a way that helps you better tell the stories you want to share. I love this photo (above) of my husband walking my son to school. If I weren't a scrapbooker, I'm not sure I would have thought about snapping that shot.

START WITH A STORY

The journaling on your layouts is like the heart of the page. After all, the reason you scrapbook is because there's some detail, experience or emotion you want to capture and preserve. So how do you start with a story? You find one! Browsing through your photo files will often encourage stories to come to life. For example, seeing an old photo of your son with his Legos may remind you that he's always been an inventor. Paying attention to what people say or do throughout the day will reveal stories as well. Perhaps your spouse mentions something in passing that sparks an insight into your family dynamics. Once you have a story established, search for photos that support the words. So many stories are waiting to be told. As you practice focusing on the story first, you'll find that the number of layouts driven by stories will grow.

Birthdays were big deals when I was growing up. We had a set of traditions that occured each year. We got to pick the menu for dinner and breakfast as well as getting served breakfast in bed - we didn't have to do any of our usual jobs. After dinner we got to eat homemade birthday cake - preceded of course by blowing out candles and making secret wishes. Now that I am a mother - I have continued the same three core traditions with my personal favorite being - eating cake.

I was looking back at the very few photos I have from my childhood, and I was struck by a photo of me with a birthday cake. I was reminded of the feeling of anticipation I had as a child, preparing to make a wish. That is the story I wanted to share on this layout. The idea was sparked by a photo, but it's the story that became the starting point for the page. So I wrote out my thoughts; my journaling talks about feeling special on my birthday and what that meant for me growing up. Only then did I search for the remaining photos and bright, cheery products that would illustrate the story.

Supplies: patterned paper (Scenic Route, Sassafras Lass); letters, rub-ons, circle accent (American Crafts); pen (EK Success)

Quick Tip

When working with photos from different time periods, trim away any distracting background elements to maintain the focus on the subject. Copy your photos if you don't want to cut the originals.

START WITH PRODUCT

Most scrappers, when they shop for scrapbook supplies, are struck by the urge to drop everything immediately and go home and create. Inspiring products can do that; they can direct our creativity and motivate us to scrapbook. Take advantage of that by allowing your page-building process to be product-guided every now and then. It could be a sheet of themed title stickers that inspires you to make an all-about-me layout, or it could be kitchen-themed paper that gives you the idea to make a recipe album. Of course, it's a good idea to spend most of your time selecting products that you have plans to use. But it's also okay to choose products just because they appeal to you even if you have no idea how you'll use them in the future. It's important to have items in your stash that will motivate you to start a page.

I collected the cheery products used on this layout and couldn't wait to put them to use! I selected spring photos that matched the brightly hued papers. With all the colors, I needed to reduce visual clutter and did so by grouping the photos on a large photo mat. The striped patterned paper directs the eye to the photos, title and journaling. I enjoyed playing with the colors and simple patterns (I had a smile on my face the whole time), but, more importantly, they support the photos and the story.

Supplies: cardstock (DCWV); patterned paper, brads (My Mind's Eye); letters (My Little Shoebox); flowers (Creative Imaginations); Misc: Segoe Print

Using Page Kits for Easy Assembly

One way to start a layout and finish it quickly is to start with a page kit. Page kits contain all the products needed to create a layout and usually include a visual of how to assemble the page. They are often sold in themes such as birthday girl, baby boy, beach vacation or high school graduation. Page kits are sold at local scrapbook and craft stores, or you can find kit clubs online.

For the layouts on the following pages, Amber Packer used the page kit July Possibilities by A Page 4 All Seasons (which is shown above each layout). You can see how complex each layout looks, yet by following the page kit design, they were a snap to build.

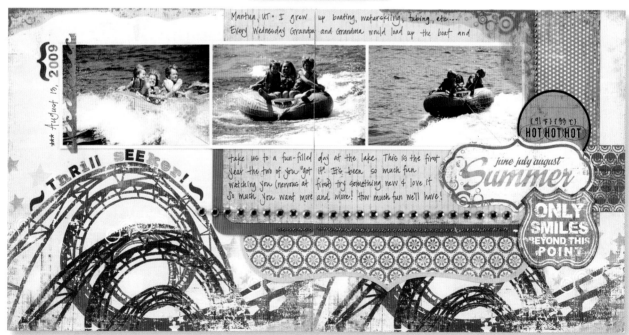

Supplies: All products from A Page 4 All Seasons

Artwork by Amber Packer

Supplies: All products from A Page 4 All Seasons

Artwork by *Amber Packer*

Basic Design Principles

Once you have a starting point, it's time to design! It's well worth your time to learn and understand the design principles as they relate to scrapbook pages. Not only will you gain knowledge, but you will be able to discern what you like and don't like visually. It can be challenging to combine photos, patterned paper, accents, text and more on one surface. Learning about design will help you through that process. I'll cover the following design principles: white space, focal point, use of shape and patterns, visual triangle, consistent margins, color, mood, repetition and balance. These basic principles will remain important and relevant no matter how advanced you become as a scrapbooker.

White Space

You don't want to fill a layout edge to edge with photos, words and product. Having too much on a page is overwhelming to the eye and distracts from the story. Your photos and stories will have the most impact when surrounded by a cushion of what's called white space. White space doesn't have to be white and it doesn't have to be expansive. It does allow for at least some empty space of breathing room on the page.

Though simple, this photo communicates much about my niece Avery. Life is changing for this mature sixth grader. She is the oldest of five, attends a school for high IQ kids, writes stories and poems almost daily and allows me to take her picture. Using just one photo allowed me to keep the layout streamlined and simple and to focus on the story. The white space supplies the neccessary breathing room on the page.

Supplies: cardstock (Bazzill); letters (American Crafts); accents (KI Memories); brad (Doodlebug Designs); pen (EK Success)

Focal Point

Every layout will have something that draws the eye first, whether you intend it or not. This is the focal point of the page. Rather than just letting it happen, use your skills to define and draw attention to the focal point of your choice. You can draw attention to a focal-point photo or other element by making it the largest item on the page. You can also draw attention by making it bolder or setting it off with color, by placing it in the upper-left corner (where the eye naturally starts) or by adding directional devices that point to it.

This layout is communicating a sequence of events: My son Justin is playing with a baby and as the photos continue, the baby is finally content holding a chunk of Justin's hair. I placed the first photo in the sequence at the upper left of the layout, where the eye naturally starts. A colorful photo mat also draws attention to it. The patterned paper with a slight arrow shape serves to highlight the last photo in the sequence.

Supplies: patterned paper (Adornit); stickers (Fiskars); letters (Doodlebug Design); pen (American Crafts)

Shape

In scrapbooking, there's one dominant shape that tends to rule all the rest: the rectangle. Photos are almost always rectangular, and most layouts are too. But variety is the spice of life, so really pay attention to how you can bring in other shapes (like circles, curves and starbursts) to contrast with all the right angles on the page. Imagine how boring the world would be without the vast array of shapes around us daily. Make sure your layouts showcase that variety too.

This layout about two little girls cheering on their older brothers playing baseball is both girly and playful. Lain utilized shape by cropping the photos into circles, which draws attention to the action in the photos and keeps the eye moving across the page. Notice how the circles are repeated in the brad accents and the decorative border along the bottom—all work together to achieve a playful design.

Supplies: patterned paper (MAMBI); letters (American Crafts); brads (Creative Imaginations); pen (American Crafts); circle template (Crafter's Workshop)

Artwork by *Lain Ehmann*

The use of bold triangles on this dinosaur-themed layout reinforces the lumpy bumpy feel of dinosaurs. This illustrates the ideal situation to introduce bold shapes: when the shapes both add interest and reinforce the theme. In addition, the chunky chipboard letters grouped together in a title that is a play on words grabs your attention and shares the mischievous mood of the outing.

Supplies: cardstock (Bazzill); patterned paper, letters (Scenic Route); stickers (Karen Foster); pen (Micron)

Artwork by *Angie Lucas*

Remember **This**

It's common to fall into the trap of setting impossible standards for yourself. If you find yourself looking for that perfect sticker to go with a layout design, and you're unwilling to scrapbook those photos until you find it, you could soon become paralyzed by indecision and insecurity. Worrying that a page won't be good enough is the quickest way to drive the fun right out of the hobby. There will never be the perfect paper or accent or trim, so just relax and enjoy.

Patterns

With its color and prints, patterned paper is an essential element in page design. It works to enhance the mood or theme of a page. For example, you can add to the silly mood of a layout with playful geometric patterns or enhance a romantic page with a small floral motif. Take care when using patterns, however, because without care, they can distract from photos.

BASIC PATTERNS

You are surrounded by them: stripes, polka dots, diamonds, grids. Because they are basic and their impact is minimal, these familiar patterns work well in most designs. They couple well with bolder prints and keep the focus on the photos.

Polka dot and striped patterned paper is a fail-proof combination for any layout. The patterned paper on this layout has a more sophisticated color palette that works with the theme of adult friendships. Distressed edges give the paper a worn feel that blends well with the vintage-inspired floral accents. Journaling is handwritten to represent the simplicity of friendships.

Supplies: cardstock (Prism); patterned paper, stickers (7Gypsies); flowers (Making Memories, Fancy Pants); trim, tickets (Making Memories); pen (EK Success); Misc: brads

ORGANIC PATTERNS

These patterns mimic shapes that are derived from nature. While the patterns on a paper are repetitive, the scale and placement are varied to replicate the look of nature where nothing is exact. The benefit of working with this type of pattern is it will complement a more relaxed design.

Using photos of the same subjects taken a few months apart, this layout is all about a little girl who adores her older cousin (and vice versa). The soft pinks couple with the more masculine organic prints (wood grain papers and chipboard accents) to complement the subjects' relationship.

Supplies: patterned paper, chipboard, border stickers (Pink Paislee); letters (Bo Bunny, Pink Paislee); pen (Stampin' Up!); Misc: chipboard button

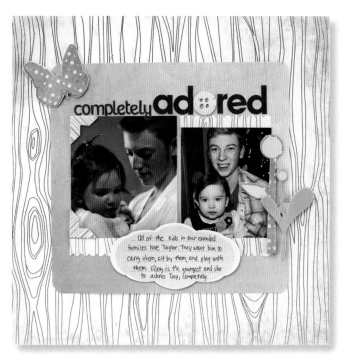

ABSTRACT SHAPES

Abstract shapes have elements that are familiar (like lines and curves) but they are undefined, unlike standard shapes such as circles and squares. As with organic shapes, this type of pattern complements a relaxed design as well as a modern one.

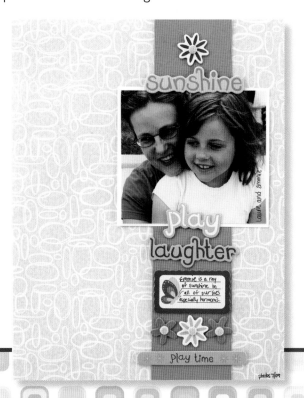

I snapped this photo of my sister and her daughter while they were watching a parade. I love the way their faces are snuggled next to each other in an intimate way. No other photos were necessary to communicate the special relationship. To offset the abstract patterned background, I used a strong vertical line to mat the photo, title, journaling and accents. The strip also works to ground the elements and guide the eye away from the busy background and toward the photo.

Supplies: patterned paper (Adornit); chipboard accents (KI Memories); brads (Doodlebug Design); pen (American Crafts)

Visual Triangle

A visual triangle is a guide for placing accents and/or colors on a page. To complete a visual triangle, pick one spot and place two more accents (or groupings of accents) to form a triangle. A triangle works because it draws your eye around the page and provides cohesion for the separate elements.

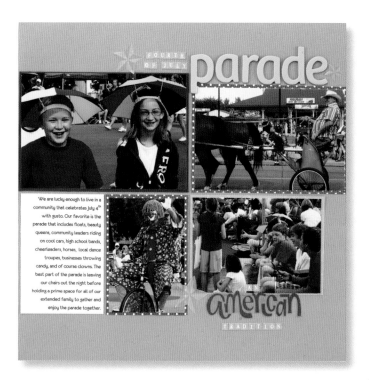

With all the movement and color going on in these photos, it was important to keep the design's colors and accents to a minimum, and that they serve to support the theme of the layout. Placing the yellow star stickers in a triangle balances the layout and keeps the viewer's eye moving throughout the page. Overlapping the stickers on the photos and background also serves to ground the elements and connect the pieces.

Supplies: cardstock (Bazzill); patterned paper (Daisy Bucket Designs); letters (Pink Paislee, Adornit); stickers (EK Success); Misc: Euroference font

The use of soft colors and gentle patterns plays up the theme of this sweet baby layout. The strategic placement of the epoxy accents guides the eye to see all elements of the layout. Placing them in a visual triangle is both pleasing to the eye and keeps the accents from overwhelming the layout. You may be tempted to use all of the stickers or accents that come on a sheet. Opt to use just three instead, and group them in a triangle for instant design success.

Supplies: patterned paper (Pink Paislee, Little Yellow Bicycle); journaling paper, epoxy accents (Little Yellow Bicycle); letters (October Afternoon, Making Memories); pen (EK Success)

Consistent Margins

Using consistent margins—whether photos and elements are butted up to one another or given space to breathe—provides a page with a polished look. No matter what the size of the margins, keeping them consistent will balance out a busy design or enhance a simple one.

Wondering how thorough your road trip layout can be with just five photos? Very—with photos of the people who went, places you saw and notes about the highlights. Notice that in addition to consistent margins between photos, the margins on all four sides of the layout are also similar in size. Using consistent margins allows you to keep a design simple.

Supplies: cardstock (American Crafts); letters (Scenic Route); number sticker (Making Memories); button (American Crafts); pen (Sakura)

Artwork by *Angie Lucas*

This brightly colored layout reminds me of a lively trip to Olvera Street in Los Angeles. With all the color and action in the photos, this layout's design lends itself well to utilizing consistent margins. I generally eyeball my margins, placing the photo nearest the center first and working around it. All the elements here fit neatly together.

Supplies: cardstock (Prism); patterned paper, stickers (October Afternoon); letters (American Crafts); pen (Sakura)

Color

You can manipulate the perception of your layouts by strategically using colors. Perhaps you want to evoke romance. Use soft hues of pink and red. Be fearless when it comes to using color, keeping in mind that the colors you choose also work to highlight photos or distract from them. Use the colors around you to draw inspiration—select hues in catalogs, packaging, clothing, fabric, home décor and anything else that catches your eye.

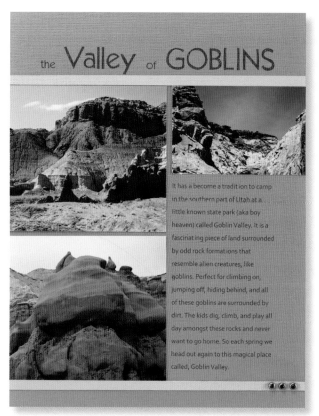

I wanted to draw viewers into the amazing detail in these desert photos. To do that, I used cardstock that matched the colors in the photos. The proportions of the two colors, mostly rust and a little bit of blue, mimic the proportions in the photos. The colors are distinct to the physical location of where the photos were taken, so they enhance the story. Plus, sticking with basic cardstock and just a few brads brought the layout together quickly.

Supplies: cardstock (Bazzill); brads (American Crafts); Misc: Positv-A and Corbel fonts

The photo on this layout has lots of colors but no strong theme (despite the Christmas tree in the background). Sticking with the traditional red and green colors unites the photo with the holiday products for a great layout with a clear theme. Using products from a coordinated line makes color matching easy.

Supplies: cardstock (Bazzill); patterned paper, letters, chipboard buttons (Making Memories); Misc: ribbon, pen

MONOCHROMATIC COLOR SCHEME

A monochromatic scheme uses one color in varying intensities. This color scheme works with any topic, regardless of theme, and maintains a classic look. It also makes coordinating colors simple, since you are deadling with just one.

Going for a happy mood, I selected orange for this monochromatic page about my son and his cousin. It took no time at all to pull the accents together since I limited my choices to just one color. Adding black-and-white journaling stickers works because the photos are also black and white. All of these colors together make for a smart, simple layout.

Supplies: cardstock (Prism); patterned paper (Cosmo Cricket); flowers, button (Sassafras Lass); stickers (American Crafts); letters (BasicGrey); pen (American Crafts)

Remember **This**

Trying to select the ideal colors can be frustrating and time-consuming. Select colors that you are drawn to, colors you would like to surround yourself with. Color is subjective, and while it's nice to coordinate the colors of your layout with the colors of your photos, this is not the only way to use color. Once you have colors you like, add photos and create. You're sure to be pleasantly surprised by the results.

Mood

Mood is the feeling behind the layout. For example, if you were scrapping birthday photos, you'd likely want the mood to be happy. To communicate that happines, you would use elements like bright colors, friendly shapes and sparkle. Compare the two layouts below. Which one communicates a celebratory mood?

These two layouts are telling the same exciting story—that of getting a driver's license. One uses dynamic bright product to communicate the thrill and the second uses muted colors and traditionally styled design. Which one betters suits the theme and mood? The layout titled "Drive." Not only are the colors bright, the nontraditional font, the silver star and brightly colored ribbons enhance the excitement of the topic.

Supplies: cardstock (Bazzill); journaling stickers (Heidi Swapp); chipboard letters (Bo Bunny); number stickers (American Crafts)

Supplies: cardstock (Bazzill); patterned paper (Sassafras Lass); letters (American Crafts, Making Memories); ribbon (American Crafts)

Repetition

Implementing repetition in design simply means duplicating some design element on a layout, for example, repeating colors in a photo and background paper or repeating specific shapes. Using this principle allows you to simplify your design decisions and make the design cohesive.

Basic chipboard accents enhnace numerous themes and designs—I customized these accents with primary colored, school-themed patterned paper to match the field trip photos. Notice how I used them to create repetition on the page. The patterned paper is repeated in the background and on the arrow accents. The theme is also repeated with the photos and the products.

Supplies: cardstock (American Crafts); patterned paper (Scenic Route); letters (Karen Foster); arrows (Bazzill); pen (American Crafts)

Customize Chipboard Accents for Any Theme

Plain chipboard is meant for customizing. You can paint, ink, chalk or cover the shapes with patterned paper to coordinate with any layout. It's also great for bringing elements of a page together using repetition: just cover multiple pieces with the same patterned paper.

MATERIALS LIST
pencil, chipboard shapes, patterned paper, small scissors or craft knife, glue stick, sandpaper or emery board

1. With a pencil, lightly trace the chipboard shape on patterned paper. Make sure both the paper and the shape are facing up.

2. Cut out the shape out using micro-tip scissors or a craft knife. Then adhere the paper shape to the chipboard shape with a glue stick.

3. With a small emery board or piece of sandpaper, lightly sand the edges of the paper until they are smooth and even with the chipboard edges. File a bit more if you want a distressed look.

Balance

When life is balanced, you feel calmer, more organized and content. Balance in layout design works much the same way. In order to create an appealing layout, you need to achieve visual balance on the page. There are two types of balance: one is symmetrical, where everything has an opposite so it is balanced in an obvious way. The second is asymmetrical, in which elements offset each other.

From the vertical title to the bright flourishes, this action-packed layout tells the story of a dad who enjoys spending time with his kids. The elements work together to achieve a balanced and lively layout. Notice how the green trim and patterned paper ground the photos, giving the layout a foundation. The title is the first element the eye sees, then it's guided around the page to the photos and to the journaling labels. The yellow patterned paper strip balances out the yellow stickers that adorn the photos.

Supplies: cardstock (American Crafts); patterned paper (Paper Salon); letters, buttons, stickers (American Crafts); pen (EK Success); Misc: tags

Remember **This**

Knowing the rules means you can break them from time to time. If you feel like creating an off-balance layout, go right ahead! There aren't any scrapbooking police that will arrest you for breaking the rules.

SYMMETRICAL BALANCE

Symmetrical balance, as you probaly guessed, involves symmetry—one side is the same as the other (much like a balanced scale). If you were to fold a symmetrically balanced layout in half, the placement of the elements on one side would look very much like the other.

The pairing of colors and photos works to infuse a feeling of glee—that feeling that comes from being surrounded by your favorite things. As you can see, the design is quite symmetrical, with a square photo collage centered in the background. The symmetrical design supports the photos by allowing the visual interest to come from the objects in the photos themselves rather than the background design. In addition, the title balances out the journaling block.

Supplies: cardstock (Prism); patterned paper (Scenic Route); heart stickers (MAMBI); letters (Pink Paislee); journaling sticker (American Crafts); button (Sassafras Lass); pen (EK Success)

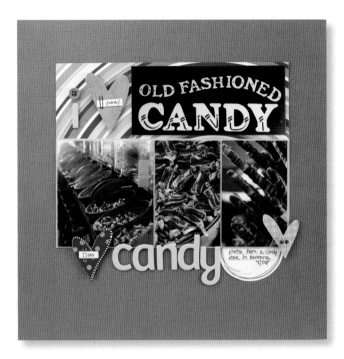

ASYMMETRICAL BALANCE

Asymmetrical balance is uneven, however the layout's elements are still visually balanced. Think of a tall tree next to a park bench. The tree is stronger visually because of its size, however the bench does not seem out of place because it enhances the scene. That is how the elements used in an asymmetrical design can work: One might be dominant, but the others still make sense on the page, working to balance the design.

The subject in the focal point photo has her head tilted so your eye looks to the start of the title and continues looking all around the rest of the layout. The two-part title is equal in weight to the two photos and the placement of both work to create an asymmetrical design.

Supplies: patterned paper, brads (Doodlebug Designs); letters (Making Memories, Heidi Swapp); circle tag (Making Memories); pen (Pilot)

Putting It All Together

You don't have to master all the design principles at once. Pick just one or two to practice and apply to layouts. Before you know it, you'll be creating successful designs without even thinking about it!

This well-designed layout features many of the design principles discussed in this chapter. The balance is symmetrical, and the bright colors liven the mood. The striped paper accents placed in a visual triangle draw the eye around the layout, to each photo, and from the title to the journaling. Consistent margins and sufficient white space provide for a clean look with room to breathe. In addition, a simple background and a black photo mat make the photos pop. I upped the style factor with playful trim and labels for journaling.

Supplies: cardstock (Bazzill); patterned paper (Scenic Route); letters (American Crafts); star die-cut (QuicKutz); label stickers (Jenni Bowlin); pen (Sharpie)

Building a Layout

So you understand what good design is—now what? How do you layer all the elements on a page and make them work together? Follow the process below to ensure building success!

MATERIALS LIST
photos, cardstock, patterned paper, journaling labels or cards, letters, adhesive, additional embellishments

1. Gather products that coordinate with the photos you will scrap: background cardstock, patterned paper, letters and other embellishments.

2. Determine how and where you will place the photos. I decided to place my photos on a single photo mat, so I added the page first.

3. Crop photos as needed, then arrange them on the page and attach them. Keep in mind the principle of consistent margins as you work with the photos.

4. Begin adding embellishments. Keep in mind the principle of balance as you add elements. I decided on a symmetrical balance, so I added a strip of patterned paper to make the photo block appear centered on the page.

5. Continue adding embellishments like the title and other accents. Look for ways to further the balance on the page and apply other design principles. Here, I added the title words to the top and bottom of the photo block to keep the symmetrical balance. I also added patterned paper elements to create a visual triangle using several stars to provide repetition and shape.

6. Add journaling, using either labels or blocks, or simply handwrite words on the background. Be sure to keep in mind the design as you place your journaling. Here, I placed the journaling over the photos to draw in the eye.

Utilizing Sketches

Think of a layout sketch as a blueprint or map for your page design. It includes information about the size and placement as well as location of other design elements and journaling. Some sketches are more detailed than others, but they all provide a no-fail approach to design. You can find sketches in many scrapbooking books, online and in the scrapbooking magazines. (And be sure to check out the gallery of sketches on pages 120–123.)

How to Use a Sketch

As I mentioned, a sketch is like a blueprint for the design. Take a look a the placement of elements on a sketch and use that as a guide for how to place the elements on your layout. There are no rules with sketches—follow them exactly or rotate them, eliminate elements or change the size of the photos. The layouts on these two pages show how you can use the same sketch multiple times to create layouts with completely different styles and moods. Plus, you can use the sketches here and on the following pages to inspire your own layouts!

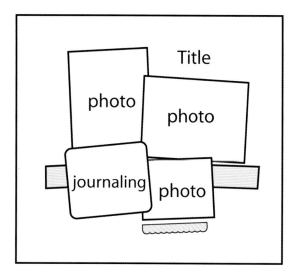

My husband Kent's favorite solitary pastime is fly-fishing with his dog by his side, so I captured that on this layout. Using masculine patterns and the three best photographs I had helped capture the story of contentment. Following the sketch, I overlapped the emebllishment in the center to connect all of the pieces, thereby making the design feel complete.

Supplies: cardstock (American Crafts); patterned paper (Bo Bunny, BasicGrey); letters (K&Co.); stickers (Adornit); pen (Stampin' Up!)

Quick Tip

Collect your favorite sketches in a binder or folder for easy reference.

As you can see, just switching the products provides a whole new look based on the same sketch (seen on the previous page). Changing the background paper to a sprightly blue and adding a touch of glitter changes the mood from calm to celebratory. With a strong focal point photo and two supporting shots, this layout effectively shares the story. Sticker trim grounds the photos and unifies the elements.

Supplies: cardstock (DCWV); patterned paper (My Little Shoebox, American Crafts); die-cut letters (QuicKutz)

Quick Tip

Becky Fleck's books *Scrapbook PageMaps* and *Scrapbook PageMaps 2* each offer sixty sketches (and more than one hundred layout ideas) plus take-along cards for shopping and scrapping on the go. You'll also find sketches of all sizes on her Web site, www.pagemaps.com.

Starting with a sketch helps you quickly decide how many photos are going to be included on your layout. The sketch below allows for three photos—two that are sized the same and a third that is smaller. When selecting photos, make sure that the larger photos portray the focus of the story, while the smaller ones provide detail.

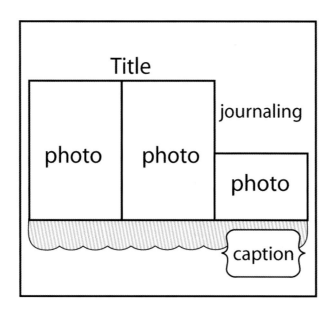

The decorative border underlining the photos communicates the playful nature of this animal lover's layout. As you read the title across the top it guides you to the journaling. A nice package—so nice, in fact, that I tried this sketch out on a second set of vertically oriented photos. You should do the same!

Supplies: cardstock (Prism); letters (Colorbok); chipboard accents, button (American Crafts); pen (EK Success)

Due to its simplicity—with a linear row of photos, a title that sits on the top and journaling shaped in a column—this sketch is one you can use time and time again. To start a layout using this sketch, place three same-sized photos that span the width of the page. Your title can be long or short, depending on your needs. Want to dress it up? Add decorative elements to the border and around the journaling.

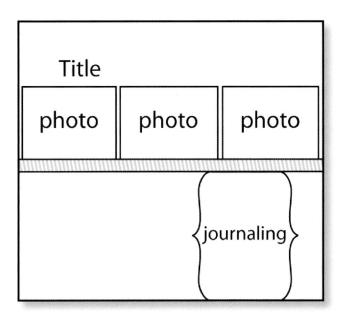

Consider taking photos of your everyday life. At the time I took these photos, it was winter so I was enjoying soup and reading during the cold winter nights. I had three telephones, which shows how busy my life was. The sketch above suited the unfussy look I was going for. Since then, my life has changed, so I am extra glad I took the time to scrapbook those days.

Supplies: patterned paper, paper trim (Sassafras Lass); letters (Making Memories); journaling paper (Scenic Route); pen (EK Success)

Double-Page Layouts

Single-page layouts are the most typical and simplest to start with when learning to design a page. But when you are feeling more comfortable designing pages and are working with lots of photos, consider crafting a double-page layout. Double-page layouts usually consist of two 12" × 12" (30cm × 30cm) pages, but other sizes work as well. With two pages side by side that act as one large canvas, this type of layout gives you lots of room for photos. Though the canvas is larger, you should employ the same design principles you would use on a single page. Below are a few tips that will help ensure that the two pages in your double layouts are unified.

Add a Large Photo Mat

You can unify a collage of photos on two pages by placing them on one large photo mat.

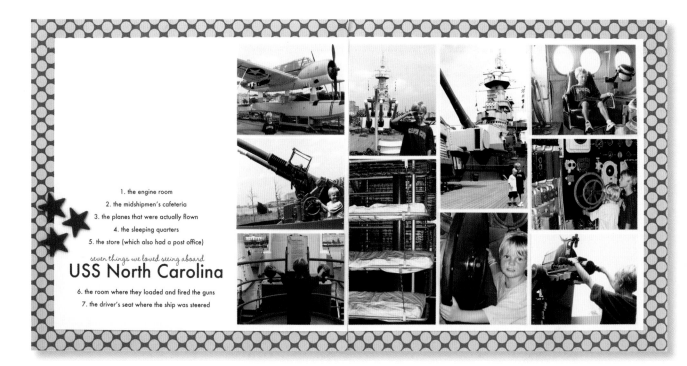

When scrapbooking an outing, you are bound to have a large selection of photos. Of course, your first job is to edit these down to the ones that capture the experience best, as Beth did with these photos. This layout shows how using a large mat to frame a photo collage unites a double-page layout. Using the same patterned background provides connection as well. Also, note Beth's use of consistent margins and white space.

Supplies: patterned paper (K&Co.); Misc: stars, Amelie and Futura fonts

Artwork by *Beth Proudfoot*

Use the Same Paper and Elements

Whether solid or patterned, select the same paper to use as the background on each page of the layout. This makes it obvious that the pages belong together. Also, repeat design elements—like shapes, colors and embellishments—from the first page onto the second page.

Using the same blue cardstock for the background reinforces the cohesiveness of this double-page layout. And with the horizontal placement of the photos (and the split title, which I'll discuss on the next page), the eye is drawn from the first page to the next. In addition, I repeated elements on both sides of the seam to connect the pages: glittery fall leaves, buttons and patterned paper make appearances on both pages and support the cozy fall theme.

Supplies: cardstock (Bazzill); patterned paper, letters (BasicGrey); leaves (Scenic Route); buttons (Autumn Leaves); punch, pen (Stampin' Up!)

Cross the Seam

Another way to unite a double-page layout is to place photos or other elements across the seam. Straddling elements will draw the eye swiftly from one page to the next. You'll need to cut photos to place them across the seam, so watch where you separate them to avoid slicing a person's face in half or cropping an important subject. When splitting titles, simply place the seam in a space between words (as I did on "Thompson's Cabin" on the previous page).

The great thing about a double-page layout is that you can fit standard-sized photos with ease. On this layout about my son's ninth birthday, I split two of the photos over the seam to help unite the pages. In addition, I used the same background and repeated the orange elements on both pages. The touches of patterned scraps provide pops of color, and bold die-cut letters make a stand-out title. To make the 9 stand out even more, I attached it with dimensional adhesive. Here's a tip for connecting a group of photos without using a mat: Add large photo corners instead. I also recommend taking lots of photos of birthday cake—they're a great way to infuse festivity into a birthday layout.

Supplies: cardstock (DCWV); patterned paper (My Little Shoebox, American Crafts); die-cut letters (QuicKutz)

Bridge the Gap—Split Photos over a Seam

As you know by now, splitting a photo over a double-page spread unifies the two pages. Splitting a photo is easier said than done, but with some quick tips, you can create a flawless double page.

MATERIALS LIST
photos, adhesive, paper trimmer

1. Place your background pages side by side and flush with each other. Place the photos where you want them over the seam. Attach the photos to just the left page.

2. Flip the pages over to the back. Add adhesive to the photos that hang off the edge of the page. Then attach the other page to the photos.

3. Turn the pages back over to the front. Cut the pages apart along the seam, right through the photos.

Design Principles Checklist

Practice makes perfect! Use this checklist to keep track of the design principles you've applied to layouts and discover which ones you prefer.

- ☐ focal point
- ☐ white space
- ☐ shape
- ☐ patterns
- ☐ visual triangle
- ☐ consistent margins

- ☐ color
- ☐ monochromatic color
- ☐ mood
- ☐ repetition
- ☐ symmetrical balance
- ☐ asymmetrical balance

Principles I prefer: _____

Principles I need to practice: _____

Chapter Five

Playing With Themes

Now that we've covered the essentials of the craft, you have the knowledge to branch out on your own and make your way through the wide world of scrapbooking. The great thing about scrapbooking is that there are few rules, and you can frame any layout around any theme you choose. But with all the options before you, deciding where to start can be a challenge. With that in mind, I've put together a gallery of themed layouts to give you some inspiration for the types of layouts you're likely to create first. Plus, now that you have a foundation of basic techniques, I've included some additional techniques for you to expand your knowledge and enhance your page designs (and enhance your fun!). Try them as described or allow yourself to experiment. Remember, the ultimate rule in scrapbooking is to have fun and do what's best for you.

Theme Ideas

When you're starting out, a few layout themes pop up often:

- babies, kids and pets
- birthdays and special occasions
- family time and relationships
- vacations and trips
- holidays and seasons

On the following pages is a gallery of layouts ideas. As you flip through, understand that you can translate any one of these layout designs into a different theme. And you can take elements from multiple layouts and combine them on your own unique page.

Babies, Kids and Pets

Change is a constant in our lives and it is especially apparent in children, which is probably why we take so many photos of our kids. Surrounded by zillions of pictures, it's easy to get lost and overwhelmed, but remember, you are the one telling the story and have the power to pick the images to illustrate it. Along with photos of little ones, make sure to include layouts about older kids and furry friends.

Use brightly colored papers and elements to establish a sense of carefree fun on a pet-themed layout. Mount photos with a neutral color, especially if you're using color photos, to avoid competition between the photos and paper. For pizazz, frame the page with a thin patterned paper border as I did here.

Supplies: patterned paper (Sassafras Lass); letters (My Little Shoebox); journaling card (Jillibean Soup); Misc: brads, label

Remember **This**

Scrapbooking is supposed to be fun and creative. Sometimes you just need to cut a frame freehand or journal without lines to maintain the fun of scrapbooking. Avoid getting caught up in perfection!

Conveying a sense of peace and quiet is easy. Simply choose soft, sweet accents for your layout such as lace trim, rounded corners, flowers and a scalloped border. Rachel developed a focal point on this layout by placing an element next to the largest photo. Notice how the tab offsets the three flower accents and gives the eye a natural line to follow.

Supplies: patterned paper, trim, flowers, tab (Making Memories); Misc: decorative scissors

Artwork by *Rachel Gainer*

Our first night together, I got up a dozen times to make sure you were still breathing. Your breaths were so gentle that I didn't trust my eyes or my ears, so I put one arm along each side of your body and squeezed just a bit to make you squeak and adjust. Only then was I satisfied that you were safe and sound. Since I'd always been a heavy sleeper, I also worried I wouldn't wake up to your cries. But fortunately, Heavenly Father blessed me with "mommy ears," and at the slightest movement or sound, I was wide awake and at your side. Usually a light sleeper, your daddy slept soundly, even asking on occasion, "Did Shelby sleep through the night?" Nope, he just didn't wake up. I guess he was blessed with "daddy ears," which made it much easier for him to get up early and go to work.

Surrounding a black-and-white photograph with brightly colored patterned papers draws the eye toward the photo and up to the title, communicating the subject of the layout. For creative journaling, place lengths of paper an equal distance apart and write in the spaces between the papers. Finally, set everything at an angle to spice things up.

Supplies: cardstock (Archivers); patterned paper (Sassafras Lass, Scenic Route, Tinkering Ink); letters (Doodlebug Designs); brads (American Crafts); pen (Micron)

Artwork by *Emily Pitts*

Since this layout is all about my niece Emmie and her happy nature, I used bright colors and feminine patterned paper. I chose two photos of Emmie and in each of them she is making eye contact, which draws attention to her sunny disposition. I jazzed up the patterned paper, highlighting parts with a pen and dressing the flower centers with rhinestones and colored brads, capturing the essence of Emmie's sparkling personality. The bit of circular patterned paper is positioned to look like a rainbow. Note how I softened the overall look by rounding the corners of the photo mat and journaling block.

Supplies: cardstock (Bazzill); patterned paper (Scenic Route); brads (Doodlebug, SEI, KI Memories, Making Memories); pen (EK Success)

Dress Up Patterned Paper

Give plain patterned paper a little flair with some easy details. All you need are a pen and tiny accents to enhance a plain design.

MATERIALS LIST
patterned paper, colored pen (or glitter glue), paper piercer, brads, buttons, pearls and/or rhinestones

1. Trace around parts of the patterned paper design using a colored pen. For even more pizazz use glitter glue instead.

2. Pierce holes for brads in various places in the pattern. In a floral pattern, brads make great flower centers. Insert the brads.

3. Adhere buttons, rhinestones, pearls and/or other small embellishments to the patterned paper.

My children inherited a trait from their maternal grandfather: long eyelashes. Wanting to scrapbook this physical feature in my son Caden, I gathered a handful of photos that showed off his lashes. I trimmed the photos to focus on the eyes and placed them in a line, adding embellishments around them. Finally, I used dimensional adhesive to add depth to the hand-cut letters.

Supplies: cardstock (Bazzill); patterned paper (Cosmo Cricket); letter stickers (Adornit); chipboard, pin accent (American Crafts); journaling card (Autumn Leaves); pen (Sakura)

Even big kids should star on layouts. You can incorporate memorabilia for kid-themed layouts as a part of the background, like Katrina did with the copy of a soccer schedule. Pair memorabilia with a touch of colorful patterned paper and include small photos of items, like trophies. Note how the rounded corners at the bottom soften the layout just a bit.

Supplies: cardstock (DCWV); patterned paper (American Crafts); letters (American Crafts)

Artwork by *Katrina Simeck*

Nate is normally the brave one, he will go first when no one else will, he calls people on the phone he doesn't know, and he doesn't mind going to new peoples houses. He is both confident and brave. When given the chance to do something new he takes it - just like these photos indicate. He was brave enough to try a front flip and he suceeded. Good job! 6/09

nate is up up in the sky

I chose this whimsical owl design, along with playful colors and patterns and a title that dances along the bottom, to represent the flying theme. Note how the dark brown background really makes the bright colors pop. Brown is a great background choice for that reason, plus it provides a softer look than black.

Supplies: cardstock (Prism); patterned paper (American Crafts); letters (Pink Paislee, Bo Bunny); pen (EK Success)

Craft Custom Embellishments With Patterned Paper

I call this technique "fussy cutting," though that may leave you thinking the work isn't worth the result. But, really, it is! Fussy cutting is simply cutting out shapes and designs from patterned paper to use as custom embellishments.

MATERIALS LIST
sharp, micro-tip scissors, patterned paper, adhesive foam

1. Cut out shapes from the patterned paper using sharp, micro-tip scissors.

2. Cut out additional, smaller shapes to layer over the shapes you cut in step 1. Attach the smaller shapes to the larger shapes using adhesive foam.

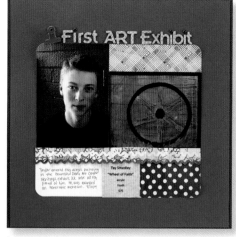

Variation
Find a patterned paper with horizontal designs to cut custom trim. Crumple the trim before placing it on the page for a added texture and dimension.

Mimicking the colors in the photo, this layout design shows off how much my niece Chloe enjoys camping. The patterns in the hat inspired the eclectic photo mat, crafted from a pile of scraps and a square punch. Each patterned square has at least one color that matches the colors in the scrap piece on the other side. That allows the patterns to mix in a cohesive yet funky manner.

Supplies: Patterned paper (October Afternoon, BasicGrey, Scenic Route, Doodlebug Designs, Making Memories, American Crafts, Cosmo Cricket); letters (American Crafts); Misc: corner rounder, square punch

Utilize Scraps in a Photo Mat

A colorful photo mat is a great way to use up some of those paper scraps you've been saving. Select several patterns that coordinate and reflect the subject matter, like the earth tones I chose for this camping layout. Don't be afraid to add a splash of color!

MATERIALS LIST
variety of patterned paper scraps, square punch, cardstock mat, corner rounder

1. Punch squares from patterned paper scraps. Turn over the punch so you can see exactly what you're punching. You'll need about 14 squares for a mat for a 4" × 6" (10cm × 15cm) photo.

2. Cut a piece of cardstock the size of your photo mat. A 5½" × 7" (14cm × 18cm) mat works well for a 4" × 6" (10cm × 15cm) photo. Adhere the squares to the perimeter of the cardstock.

3. Trim any uneven edges. Then round corners using a corner rounder. Attach the photo to the center of the mat.

Birthdays and Special Occasions

Everyone remembers to bring their cameras out for birthdays and special events. So take advantage of the camera-ready occasion, and photograph the details so you'll be ready to scrap any sort of story. For example, at a birthday party try take a photo of the pile of presents, the cake preparation and the special decorations. When selecting photos to scrapbook, look for images that encapsulate the mood of the event.

Grouping birthday photos that cover mutiple years is a fun way to watch someone grow up. It's also a simple way to scrap multiple years on one page. For a birthday layout like this, use themed patterned paper for the background to complement the photos. Crop photos to the same size for a clean design. Finish up with a quick title and a few numbers to effectively communicate the passage of time.

Supplies. cardstock (American Crafts); patterned paper (Frances Meyer, Flair Designs); letter, die-cut (Making Memories); number, pen (American Crafts)

Artwork by *Monica McNeil*

Keep wedding layouts classic, like this one, by using patterned papers with sophisticated, monochromatic designs. Choosing soft hues that match the wedding colors generates flow between the photos and pieces of the layout. For simple but meaningful journaling, use lyrics from a song—like one played at the wedding or a favorite ballad of yours.

Supplies: patterned paper (Chatterbox); flowers (Prima Marketing); Misc: French Script and Gisha fonts
Photographs by Elisha Snow

This layout about my twentieth wedding anniversary conveys a sense of love, commitment and connection. Dressing up the accents with dry embossing is both subtle and sophisticated. To make sure you get into the family scrapbooks, hand over the camera. My oldest son took this photo a week before my anniversary.

Supplies: cardstock (Bazzill); letter stickers, border stickers (Pink Paislee); heart die-cut (Provo Craft); title die-cut (QuicKutz); Misc: Studio font

Stand Out With Embossing

Embossing is a great way to provide texture and dimension without adding bulk. Heat embossing requires a heat gun and embossing powder to create tactile design fingers can't resist.

MATERIALS LIST
stamp, watermark ink or pigment ink, embossing powder, heat gun

1. Stamp the image on your background using transparent watermark ink or pigment ink (the same color as your embossing powder). These inks dry slower than dye ink, allowing enough time for the embossing to take place.

2. Sprinkle embossing powder. over the stamped image, covering it completely. Tap any excess powder back into the jar.

3. Apply heat to the powder using the heat gun. Be sure to hold the gun at least 6" (15cm) from the paper to keep from warping or scorching it. Continue to apply heat until the powder is melted and the image appears shiny.

Variation
Dry embossing transfers raised designs using templates and a machine like the Cuttlebug (by Provo Craft). You can purchase all sorts of embossing plates with images. To emboss, simply slide the template and paper into the machine and roll them through.

Family Time and Relationships

Celebrating everyday family activities and important relationships is a key part of life, so it makes sense to photograph these seemingly mundane moments and scrapbook them. You will be surprised how significant these layouts become.

Because I was working with older photos on this layout, I needed to crop abundantly to zoom in on the subjects. Thin white cardstock borders create a sense of continuity among the photos, which communicates the special relationship between young Justin and his grandpa.

Supplies: cardstock (Bazzill); patterned paper (BasicGrey); letters (American Crafts); Misc: tag, pen, brads

Cut a Perfect Photo Mat

A paper trimmer (a scrapbooker's best friend) is an essential tool for crafting perfect photo mats because of its handy measuring capabilities—you'll get a perfectly straight and even photo mat every time.

MATERIALS LIST
photo, cardstock, adhesive, paper trimmer

1. Adhere the photo to the cardstock, leaving an evenly sized border on two sides.

2. Trim the two remaining sides, using the trimmer's handy ruler guidelines.

The colorful background paper brings out the love and joy found in these photos of my kids and their Aunt Heather. To customize the accents to match, I added a wash of paint and a touch of glitter to plain chipboard flowers and letters. Everything on this layout is touching (literally) to play up the intimate nature of the photos. The accents, journaling card and title all frame the photos and draw the eye in their direction.

Supplies: patterned paper (Fancy Pants); journaling card (K&Co.); letters, brads (American Crafts); Misc: chipboard flowers

Customize Accents With Paint and Glitter

One sure way to coordinate scrapbook layouts is to customize your accents. All it takes is your imagination combined with a few products, and you're on your way to matching any theme.

MATERIALS LIST
chipboard shapes (unfinished or finished), sandpaper (optional), paint applicator, acrylic paint, glitter glue or pen

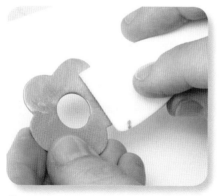

1. If you're using a finished chipboard shape, sand it before you begin. Then paint the top of the chipboard with the darker acrylic paint color using an applicator (like a makeup sponge or sponge brush).

2. Let the paint dry for a minute or two. Then apply the lighter acrylic paint color lightly. You want to achieve a transparent wash effect, so keep the application very light.

3. Let the paint dry completely. Then apply clear glitter to the chipboard using glitter glue or a glitter pen (for easy application).

Vacations and Trips

Owning a collection of fantastic photos from a once-in-a-lifetime trip is a common reason to start scrapbooking. Most people take hundreds, even thousands, of photos during travel, making this topic an ideal candidate for first layouts. Keep in mind that editing is key to designing condensed and dynamic vacation layouts. Pair your favorite memories with memorabilia for an even better perspective.

This layout contains a few photos from a fabulous trip my husband and I took to Australia and New Zealand in 2007. The travel products reinforce the theme and provide visual interest to the photos.

Supplies: cardstock (American Crafts); paper accents (Making Memories); letters (American Crafts); pen (EK Success); Misc: tags

Quick Tip

Avoid using themed product for every element in a design. Limiting themed product to just a few elements will prevent the product from overwhelming the page design.

This playful background paper lends an amusement park feel to this layout about a trip to a park in California. Inking the edges of the photo mat not only reflects the rustic mood of the photos, but also ties the photo to the red accents and the red in the background. In additon, I stacked the journaling cards, which not only coordinate with the overall quirky design but also provides ample space for recording the vacation memories I never want to forget.

Supplies: patterned paper (Cosmo Cricket); letters (American Crafts); journaling notes (Heidi Swapp); pen (EK Success)

Highlight Edges

Part of what makes scrapbooking so fun is the opportunity to play with supplies. Next time you have a layout with a solid colored background, add definition by inking or painting the edges. Use a coordinating color or try a neutral such as black, brown or white.

MATERIALS LIST
solvent or dye-based ink, acrylic paint and makeup sponge, chalk ink and cotton swab

Apply Solvent or Dye-Based Ink
Gently swipe the ink pad along the edges of the paper. Apply lightly at first, then apply more as needed.

Apply Paint
Paint will provide a thick, bold edge. Dip a makeup sponge in acrylic paint. Then lightly drag the sponge along the edges of the paper.

Apply Chalk Ink
For a soft, subtle look, apply chalk ink. Use a cotton swab to apply the chalk to the edges of the paper.

Holidays and Seasons

Holidays and seasons mark our lives so most of us take lots of photos the capture these special times. Scrapbooking events is a good starting place for new scrapbookers because you can find a large variety of products made for these themes, and you have lots of photos from which to choose.

Projecting movement on a layout is easy when you pair large action photos with swirling patterned paper. Crop your photos with a circular tool to add to the feeling of motion. If your photos are colorful, select paper that is primarily black and white with just a hint of color pulled from the photos.

Supplies: cardstock (Stampin' Up!); patterned paper, letters (American Crafts)

Artwork by *Monica McNeil*

Up close, colorful photos illustrate the sights and smells of a season and make a great focal point for a layout. For maximum impact, place your photos in a collage that spans two pages, and use a large photo mat to tie the pages together. To create a visual triangle around your photos, mat journaling and part of the title with the same color cardstock.

Supplies: cardstock (Bazzill); patterned paper (BasicGrey); letters (BasicGrey, Making Memories); brads (KI Memories); Misc: Rod font

SUMMER HIGHLIGHTS 2008

1 Chloe telling stories about kids camp 2 People watching on the Balboa Pier 3 Bandit relaxing and Caden enjoying nature at the Thompson's cabin 4 Spending time at Bear Lake with family, enjoying the beach, watching movies, and just relaxing at the cabin 5 Caden getting a summer buzz cut on our vacation 6 Shopping on Olvera Street 7 Art camp at the Dyer's 8 Camping in the beautiful Utah mountains

Show off a whole season of photos by cropping each one and placing them along the perimeter of the page like a frame. This simple way to get more photos on one page leaves room for a title and journaling in the center. Use number stickers as I did to match each photo to the appropriate journaling line.

Supplies: patterned paper, letters (Doodlebug Designs); numbers (Making Memories)

Tell a holiday story completely by simply following Elizabeth's lead. For a bit of the unexpected, place two 4" × 6" (10cm × 15cm) photos across the top of an 11" × 8½" (28cm × 21cm) page. Use up bits and pieces of different product lines by attaching each element to matching blank tags. A larger tag works well as a small space for journaling. The uniform tag shape and common theme of the products pull this adorable Halloween page together.

Supplies: cardstock (Prism); epoxy button (Making Memories); rub-ons (Fiskars); stickers (Little Yellow Bicycle, Design Originals); Misc: brad

Artwork by *Elizabeth Dillow*

When photographing a holiday event, try to get before and after shots to illustrate your subject. Using photos of different children at the same angle lends continuity to your page and makes a cute comparison. Take advantage of the empty space in photos by affixing your title to a photo using letter stickers.

Supplies: patterned paper, chipboard, stickers (KI Memories); Misc: label, Calibri font

Artwork by *Celeste Smith*

I don't think you could have been anymore excited about starting back to school. Some of the highlights of your first few days included getting your own desk, complete with your name, your own pencil box, math workbook, and eraser! Also, having Ms. Roberts again this year made the transition back to school really smooth. You are anxious already to get down to the business of learning some new things, while she is focused on getting all of you used to the new rules and routine. One week in and you love your classroom, your teacher and especially WHEE! You have been having extra recess too which is a real treat!

Photographing your child with a teacher at the beginning of the school year eases the anxieties often associated with change. It also makes for a wonderful starting point for a back-to-school layout. On this layout, the paper's design supports the theme but it's subtle enough to not overwhelm the photos. A large photo mat that frames the elements of the page ties everything together.

Supplies: patterned paper, stickers (Bo Bunny); brad (American Crafts); Misc: Teletype font

Artwork by *Celeste Smith*

To keep products from competing with the typical color-packed action photos of the holidays, try employing a white background with lots of white space. Add just a bit of traditional color that supports your theme. Use word stickers to convey the feelings and message of your layout with minimal journaling. Finally, to use a lot of photos, consider cropping each one down to just the subjects and discarding the backgrounds.

Supplies: patterned paper, stickers, words (Adornit); initial (Making Memories); pen (American Crafts)

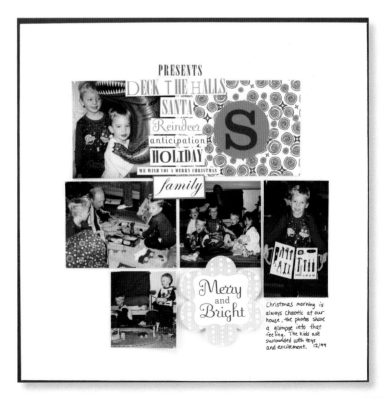

1985

the best PRESENT EVER!

joy

Paul went with my parents to Provo and I was quite jealouse. Until Christmas morning arrived and I opened my gift from Paul. It was a BYU sweatshirt - I was so surprised. I wore it through.
12/1985

Because most of the holiday accents on this page have a bright, graphic feel, distressing the background softens the overall appearance and ties the idea of opening presents to the design. Because I needed more room for the long title, I turned the layout into a landscape orientation and created a visual triangle with the circle accents to achieve balance. I also used mixed lettering styles to promote the carefree Christmas theme.

Supplies: patterned paper, letters, journaling sticker, button accent, ribbon, pen (American Crafts); epoxy sticker (Creative Imaginations)

Create a Well-Worn Look

A distressed background coordinates with contemporary and classic layout styles alike, though it works especially well with vintage photos that have their own well-worn look. This is such a quick and accessible technique you will find yourself doing it time and time again!

MATERIALS LIST
patterned paper, sandpaper or emery board

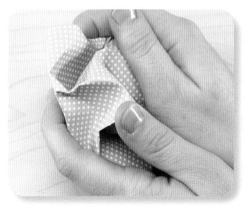

1. Gently crumple the patterned paper in your hands. Be sure to create plenty of creases.

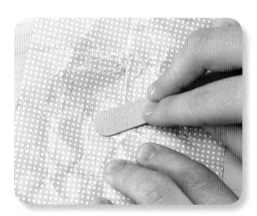

2. Flatten the paper. Then lightly sand the raised creases. If desired, sand the edges of the paper as well.

Mini Albums

For some themes you will find that you want to say more than you can on a single scrapbook layout; this is where mini albums come in handy. You can tell a complete story and include as many photos and details as you want. The selection of mini-albums—albums that are smaller than the traditional 12" × 12" (30cm × 30cm) or 8½" × 11" (21cm × 28cm)—has grown exponentially. You can find everything from sturdy albums that house your small layouts in page protectors to funky albums that have pages in different sizes and shapes. Building a design for the pages in mini albums is essentially the same as doing so for standard layouts—only on a smaller scale. When putting them together, remember your design principles and the elements of telling a good story.

Before purchasing a mini album, consider the following: Where will you house the album; will you need an album with page protectors to protect pages from little hands? Are you using standard-sized photos, thus needing a larger-sized mini album? How are you going to write the journaling? Will you need to purchase additional products? What supplies do you need to gather before you start? Will you use the same design on each page or use multiple designs? After you have considered all of these things, gather your supplies and get started!

Sticking with solid-colored background paper and bright patterned letters, this theme mini album is full of personality. Made to show off my son's double date to homecoming, this album was a breeze to build.

Supplies: album (Maya Road); cardstock (Bazzill); letters (Maya Road, Heidi Swapp); brads (Doodlebug Designs); Misc: circle punch, Bird Cherry font

Layout Sketches

Use these sketches to guide your layout designs. For more information on sketches, see pages 92–95.

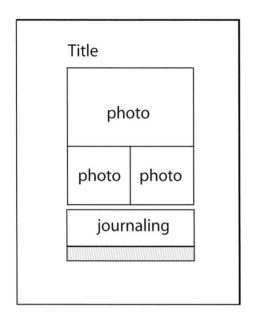

Extra, Extra!
Page 13

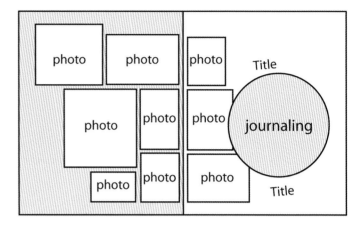

Best Friends
Page 14

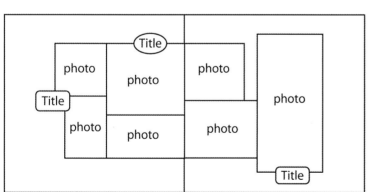

Tall Timbers
Page 42

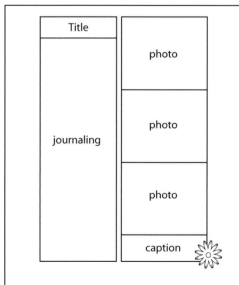

Thirty Things
Page 52

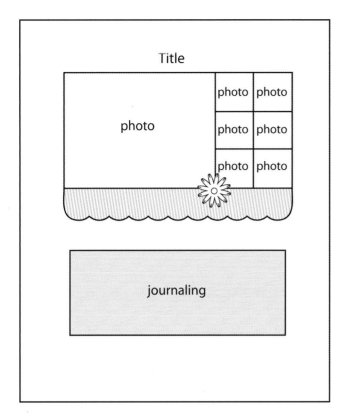

Mrs. Dyer
Page 61

Title

photo

photo | photo
photo | photo
photo | photo

journaling

Two Lil Cuties
Page 78

Title

photo | photo | photo

journaling
journaling
journaling
journaling
journaling

photo

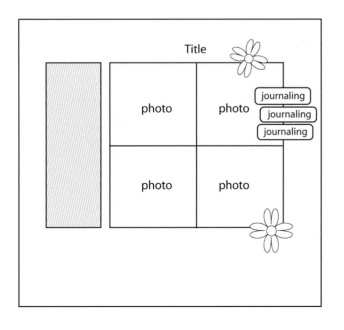

Backyard Antics
Page 90

Title

photo | photo
journaling
journaling
journaling
photo | photo

Happy
Page 92

Title

photo
photo
journaling
photo

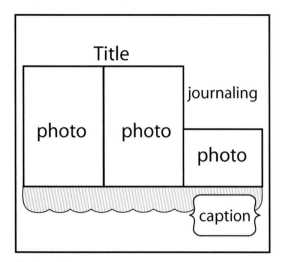

Animal Lovers
Page 94

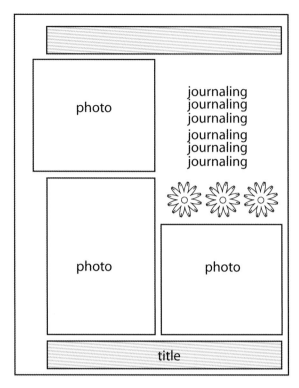

Sky
Page 106

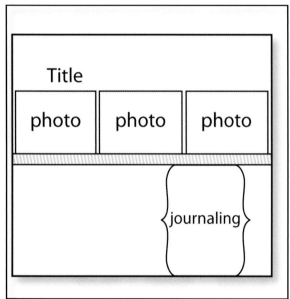

Glimpse of Today
Page 95

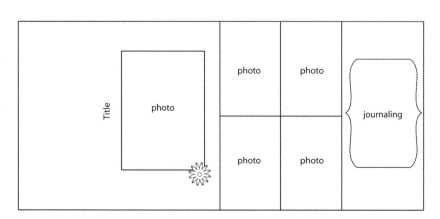

Face of Love
Page 108

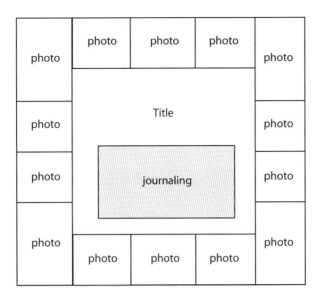

Summer Highlights
Page 115

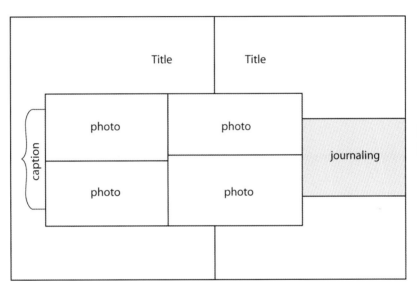

Farmer's Market
Page 114

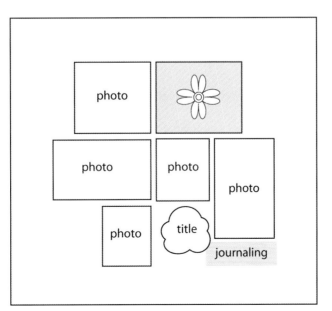

Merry and Bright
Page 117

123

Source Guide

The following companies manufacture products featured in this book. Please check your local retailers to find these materials, or go to a company's Web site for the latest product. In addition, we have made every attempt to properly credit the items mentioned in this book. We apologize to any company that we have listed incorrectly, and we would appreciate hearing from you.

100 Proof Press
(740) 594-2315
http://100proofpress.com

7Gypsies
(877) 749-7797
www.sevengypsies.com

Adornit/Carolee's Creations
(435) 563-1100
www.adornit.com

American Crafts
(801) 226-0747
www.americancrafts.com

Archivers
www.archiversonline.com

BasicGrey
(801) 544-1116
www.basicgrey.com

Bazzill Basics Paper
(480) 558-8557
www.bazzillbasics.com

BoBunny Press
(801) 771-4010
www.bobunny.com

Chatterbox, Inc.
(208) 461-5077
www.chatterboxinc.com

Colorbök, Inc.
(800) 366-4660
www.colorbok.com

Cosmo Cricket
(800) 852-8810
www.cosmocricket.com

Crafter's Workshop, The
www.thecraftersworkshop.com

Creative Imaginations
(800) 942-6487
www.cigift.com

Daisy Bucket Designs
(541) 289-3299
www.daisybucketdesigns.com

Daisy D's Paper Company
(888) 601-8955
www.daisydspaper.com

Die Cuts With A View
(801) 224-6766
www.diecutswithaview.com

Design Originals
(800) 877-7820
www.d-originals.com

Doodlebug Design Inc.
(877) 800-9190
www.doodlebug.ws

EK Success, Ltd.
www.eksuccess.com

Fancy Pants Designs, LLC
(801) 779-3212
www.fancypantsdesigns.com

Fiskars, Inc.
(866) 348 5661
www.fiskars.com

Flair Designs
(888) 546-9990
www.flairdesignsinc.com

Frances Meyer, Inc.
(413) 584-5446
www.francesmeyer.com

Graphic 45
(866) 573-4806
www.g45papers.com

Heidi Swapp/Advantus Corporation
(904) 482-0092
www.heidiswapp.com

Jenni Bowlin
www.jennibowlin.com

Jillibean Soup
(888) 212-1177
www.jillibean-soup.com/

Dèjá Views/C-Thru Ruler
(800) 243-0303
www.dejaviews.com

osolutely
wesome

u, my boy, are one of a kind. I'm not sure what
nion statement you were going for here, but we
were all laughing at your choice of tiger-print
nglasses and a too-big hat. You certainly know
how to brighten a room.

K&Company
(888) 244-2083
www.kandcompany.com

Kaiser Craft
www.kaisercraft.net

Karen Foster Design
(801) 451-9779
www.karenfosterdesign.com

KI Memories
(972) 243-5595
www.kimemories.com

Li'l Davis Designs
(480) 223-0080
www.lildavisdesigns.com

Little Yellow Bicycle - see
Dèjá Views

Luxe Designs
(972) 573-2120
www.luxedesigns.com

Making Memories
(801) 294-0430
www.makingmemories.com

Me & My Big Ideas
(949) 583-2065
www.meandmybigideas.com

Maya Road, LLC
(877) 427-7764
www.mayaroad.com

McGill, Inc.
(800) 982-9884
www.mcgillinc.com

Melissa Frances/Heart &
Home, Inc.
(905) 686-9031
www.melissafrances.com

Mustard Moon
(763) 493-5157
www.mustardmoon.com

My Little Shoebox, LLC
(510) 269-4162
www.mylittleshoebox.com

My Mind's Eye, Inc.
(800) 665-5116
www.mymindseye.com

October Afternoon
www.octoberafternoon.com

O'Scrap!/Imaginations!, Inc.
(801) 225-6015
www.imaginations-inc.com

Paper Salon
(800) 627-2648
www.papersalon.com

Pebbles Inc.
(800) 438-8153
www.pcbblcsinc.com

Pilot
www.pilotpen.com

Pink Paislee
(816) 729-6124
www.pinkpaislee.com

Prima Marketing, Inc.
(909) 627-5532
www.primamarketinginc.
com

Prism Papers
(866) 902-1002
www.prismpapers.com

Provo Craft
(800) 937-7686
www.provocraft.com

QuicKutz, Inc.
(888) 702-1146
www.quickutz.com

Rusty Pickle
(801) 746-1045
www.rustypickle.com

Sakura Hobby Craft
(310) 212-7878
www.sakuracraft.com

Sanford Corporation
(800) 323-0749
www.sanfordcorp.com

Sassafras Lass
(801) 269-1331
www.sassafraslass.com

Scenic Route Paper Co.
(801) 542-8071
www.scenicroutepaper.
com

SEI, Inc.
(800) 333-3279
www.shopsei.com

Sharpie - see Sanford

Stampin' Up!
(800) 782-6787
www.stampinup.com

Tinkering Ink
(877) 727-2784
www.tinkeringink.com

Index

Start scrapbooking great pages with ideas from these other Memory Makers Books

Remember This
Kimber McGray and Summer Fullerton

With 120 fresh layout ideas, *Remember This* will inspire you to scrap a variety of creative layouts during every season of the year. With pages featuring multiple photos, numerous styles and a variety of events and activities, plus page sketches, there's something for every scrapbooker.

ISBN-13: 978-159963-091-5; ISBN-10: 1-59963-091-5

Paperback; 128 pages; Z3842

The Scrapbook Embellishment Handbook
Sherry Steveson

Get fabulous ideas for using 17 types of embellishments, from hot materials like acrylic to old standbys like stickers and stamps. With 51 illustrated techniques and more than 120 ideas for using all kinds of embellishments, this is your go-to guide for dressing up your layouts.

ISBN 13: 978-1-59963-035-9; ISBN 10: 1-59963-035-4

Hardcover with enclosed spiral; 144 pages; Z2495

Time to Scrap
Kathy Fesmire

You'll learn through step-by-step instruction how scrapbook pages can be fast, fun, frugal and fabulous! A variety of layouts by the author and her team of contributing artists will illustrate quick techniques, plus provide additional tips and tricks for saving time and money. Includes sketches!

ISBN-13: 978-1-59963-083-0; ISBN-10: 1-59963-083-4

Paperback; 128 pages; Z2977

These books and other fine Memory Makers titles are available at your local scrapbook retailer, bookstore or from online suppliers, or visit our Web site at www.mycraftivitystore.com.

Five reasons to visit
www.memorymakersmagazine.com

1. Download FREE projects
2. Get expert advice
3. Connect with other scrappers
4. Sign up for weekly e-inspiration
5. Find the latest news, inspiration, tips and ideas